THE MYSTERIES OF WORSHIP IN ISLAM

THE MYSTERIES OF WORSHIP IN ISLAM

Translation with Commentary and Introduction

Of

AL-GHAZZALI'S BOOK OF THE IHYA' ON THE WORSHIP

EDWIN ELLIOT CALVERLEY

KITAB BHAVAN
New Delhi-110002

Kitab Bhavan
Publishers, Distributers, Exporters & Importers
1784, Kalan Mahal, Darya Ganj
New Delhi-110002 (India)

Phone : (91-11)23277392/93, 23274686
website : www.kitabbhavan.com
e-mail : nasri@vsnl.com

1st Edition : 1992
3rd Edition : 2008

ISBN : 81-7151-152-X

Published in India by:
Nusrat Ali Nasri for Kitab Bhavan
1784, Kalan Mahal, Darya Ganj
New Delhi-110002 (India)

Printed in India at:
H.S. Printers
New Delhi-110002

From the Translator's Introduction

The Muslims use the term *'ibadah* to express the relationship and attitude of a creature as slave to Allah, his Lord, Who formed him and therefore owns him. This relationship finds outward expression in acts of obedience, worship and devotion. Some of these acts are commanded; others are recommended; while still others are voluntary.

Chief among those that are commanded are fasting, pilgrimage to Mecca, payment of the quarter-tithe and the *salah. Salah* here means a specific ceremony of *ibadah,* opened with the expression "Allah is greater," and closed with the Salutation. To designate this special ceremony the term "Worship" will be used, rather than "prayer," simply because it is a ceremonial service.

It is chiefly by means of the *salah,* Worship, that the prayer and devotional life is expressed in Islam, both in public and private Worship. Other expressions of Worship and devotion consists in *al-tilawah,* the Recital of the Qur'an; *al-du'd',* the offering of Supplication; *al-dhikr,* the Invocation of the Names of Allah and the mentioning of His Qualities; *al-wird,* the Recital of a section of the Qur'an or other religious work; *al-hizb,* a Portion of the Qur'an or other devotional writing used as a petition, together with other forms of communion with Allah to be mentioned later....

The Performance of the Worship

The performance of the Worship is preceded by certain necessary acts. These include the cleansing of the body, clothing and place of Worship. Book Three of the First Quarter of the *Ihya'* describes the proper performance of these operations. After them follows the covering of the person from the navel to the knees, when the worshipper is a man. These acts are the prerequisites of the Worship.

When they are finished the man is ready for the Worship. He assumes (1) (the same numbering of the parts of the Worship will be repeated in the Analytical Table, pp. xiii-xv) the Standing Position, facing the *qiblah* with his feet apart, his head preferably inclined, and his gaze upon his place of Worship.

Then he says (2) the *Basmalah*: "In the name of Allah, the Merciful and Compassionate One," He says immediately after it (3) the *Ta'awwudh*, Seeking for Refuge: "Say: I seek refuge in the Lord of mankind, the Possessor of mankind, the God of mankind, from the evil of the Whisperer, the one who goes back, who whispers in the breasts of mankind, of the jinn and mankind" (Qur'an, cxiv.).

Then, if he expects anyone to Worship behind him, he says (4) the Call to Worship: "Allah is greater! Allah is greater! I witness. There is no god but Allah! I witness, Muhammad is the Messenger of Allah! Come to the Worship! Come to Prosperity; Allah is greater!"

Instead of the two phrases, "Come to the Worship! Come to Prosperity," called the *Hai'alatain*, the follower says: "There is no might and no strength but in Allah!"

In the Morning Worship the *mu'adhdhin* adds, after the *Hai'alatain*, the *Tathwib*: "The Worship is better than sleep!"

The follower thereupon responds: "You have spoken truly! You have acted rightly! You have given good advice!"

After the Call to the Worship, the *mu'adhdhin*, or the worshipper himself if he is alone, says (5) the Institution: "The Worship is instituted!"

The follower responds: "May Allah institute it and continue it as long as the heavens and the earth continue!"

He also adds: "O Allah! by the right of this complete Call and Worship instituted, grant Muhammad mediation and excellence, and elevate him to the praiseworthy station which Thou didst promise him: Thou dost not violate a promise!"

These items, except the Standing Position, constitute the Introduction to the Worship, and are not considered to be parts of the Worship itself. The Worship proper begins with (6) the

Intention: "I perform at its proper time the Prescribed Noon Worship to Allah."

The statement of Intention must be appropriate to the Worship presented; cf. pp. 21-22 of Translation. The Intention is made in the heart, according to al-Ghazzali. As soon as it is present in his heart, the worshipper (7) Raises the Hands, until the tips of the fingers are opposite the tops of the ears, with the palms toward the *qiblah*. Resting them there a moment, he begins (8) the *Takbir*, and then lowers his hands, placing the left just above the navel, and the right on the left, with the index and next finger along the left forearm, and the others grasping the wrist. This *Takbir* is called the *taharrum*, and also the *takbirat al-ihram*, because it forbids to the worshipper what was previously allowable, that is, he enters upon a time sacred to Allah, when only certain words and acts are allowable, and all others, at other times permissible, are now forbidden. The *Takbir* consists of the words: "Allah is greater!"

It is said by the follower only audibly enough for himself to hear, and it is said after the *imam* finishes saying it. It is immediately followed by (9) the Opening Supplication, which is so called because it is the supplication with which the Worship is begun after the *Takbir*. It is as follows: "Allah is greater indeed! Much praise belongs to Allah! O the praise of Allah, early and late! I have turned my face to Him Who divided the heavens and the earth, as a Hanif, and I am not one of the associators; my Worship and my devotion, my time of living and of dying belong to Allah, the Lord of the worlds, Who has no associate; and that I am commanded, and I am one of the Muslims."

More may be added to this. In the same position he says (10) the *Ta'awwudh*, the Seeking for Refuge: "I seek refuge in Allah from the Pelted Satan!"

Then he recites (11) the Fatihah, beginning with the *Basmalah:* "In the name of Allah, the Merciful and Compassionate One. Praise belongs to Allah, the Lord of the worlds, the Merciful Compassionator, Possessor of the Judgment Day! Thee do we Worship and of Thee do we ask aid! Guide us into the Straight Way, the Way of those on whom Thou hast bestowed favour, not of those against whom there is anger, nor of those going astray!"

It is recited audibly when alone, in the Morning, Sunset and Evening Worships. This is followed by the audible utterance of (12) the *Ta'min*: "Amin!"

Then he recites (13) the *Surah*, consisting of three or more verses of the Qur'an. At the Noon Worship the eighty-fifth *Surah* may be used, as follows: "By the sky having towers! By the Day promised! By a Seeing One, and one seen!" etc.

That finishes the Recital. The Bowing comes next. This he does by (14) Raising the Hands, and simultaneously saying (15) the *Takbir*: "Allah is greater!"

At the same time he performs (16) the Bowing, placing his palms on his knees, which are kept straight, and making his back, neck and head to be in line, level. In this position he recites, three times or, if alone, seven or ten times, (17) the *Tasbih*, or Praise: "O the praise of my great Lord!"

Then (18) he Rises to the Standing Position; (19) Raising his Hands; and says (20) the *Tasmi'*: "Allah hearkens to anyone who says His praise!"

He remains quiet a moment in this standing position.

The remaining quiet or composed is called the *tuma'innah*. While in this position he adds to the *Tasmi'*. "O our Lord! Thine is the praise to the fullness of the heavens and the earth, and to the fullness of whatever else Thou wilt!"

This may be lengthened still more in the Worships of the *Tasbih*, the Praise (see pp. 156 of the Translation) and of the *Kusuf*, Eclipse (See pp. 146 ff. of the Translation) and of the Prescribed Morning Worship. Then he lowers himself to the ground, saying (21) the *Takbir*: "Allah is greater!" until he completes (22) the Prostration, by placing his knees, hands and face on the ground. In this position he says, three or more times (23) the *Tasbih*: "O the praise of my Lord, the Most High!"

Then he (24) Raises his Head, saying (25) the *Takbir*: "Allah is greater!"

He then sits on his left foot, with his hands on his thighs, and makes (26) Seven Supplications: "O my Lord! Forgive me! Have mercy on me! Apportion provision for me! Guide me! Help me! Preserve me in health and pardon me!"

Then he lowers himself again saying (27) the *Takbir*: "Allah is greater!" and completes (28) a Second Prostration like the first, and three times (29) the *Tásbih*: "O the praise of Allah, the Most High!"

Then he raises his head, saying (30) the *Takbir*: "Allah is greater!" until he comes to the Sitting Position, sitting briefly in each *Rak'ah*, Cycle, not followed by the Witnessing, and then rises, prolonging his *Takbir* to the middle of his standing.

This is the end of the First *Rak'ah*, or cycle of acts and utterances in the Worship, and he follows it with a second, precisely like it, beginning with the Seeking Refuge.

At the end of the Second Prostration of the Second *Rak'ah*, instead of rising, the worshipper continues in (31) the Sitting Position, sitting on his left foot, with his hands on his thighs, with the index finger of the right hand extended and the others folded. Then he says (32) the First Witnessing: "The greetings belong to Allah! Peace be upon thee, O Prophet, and the mercy and blessing of Allah! Peace be upon us, and upon the righteous creatures of Allah! I witness: There is no god but Allah! I witness: Muhammad is the Messenger of Allah!"

In the same position he says (33) the Blessing upon the Messenger of Allah and upon his family: "O Allah! Bless the Messenger of Allah! and the family of Muhammad!"

Then he changes his position, and (34) sits on his left thigh, and says (35) the Last Witnessing: "I witness: There is no god but Allah! I witness: Muhammad is the Messenger of Allah!"

This is followed by (36) the Blessing upon the Prophet: "O Allah! Bless the Messenger of Allah!"

After this (37) the Traditional Supplication is said.

The worshipper may make any supplication he will for anything of this life or the next. Sayyid Murtada says the best supplication is: "O Allah! I seek refuge in Thee from the punishment of the grave! I seek refuge in Thee from the testing of the Antichrist! I seek refuge in Thee from the testing of the time of life and of death! O Allah! I seek refuge in Thee from sin and obligation!"

Then the worshipper turns his head to the right for (38) the First Salutation: "Peace be upon you, and the mercy of Allah!"

He then turns to the left for (39) the Second Salutation: "Peace be upon you, and the mercy of Allah!"

At the same time he has (40) the Intention of withdrawing from the Worship with the Salutation.

The Parts of the Worship

In the preceding description of the performance of the Worship it has been noticed that the Worship consists of acts and utterances of varying importance and prominence.

There are two preparatory operations. The first is the *wudu'*, "ablution", or *ghusl*, "bathing". This includes the cleaning of the body, clothing and place of Worship. Precise directions are given for the kind of water that may be used for the cleansing and for the *tayammum*, the use of *turab*, "clean earth," when water is not available. The other is the clothing of the person. The minimum is covering the body from the navel to the knees, for man and slave women, but the putting on of the turban is also included. The free woman covers herself as completely as she does when she is to be seen by any other people than those of her own family.

There are three other prerequisites of the Worship, which really indicate those upon whom the Worship is obligatory. These are *al-islam*, that is, acceptance of the faith, the attainment of puberty, and the possession of intelligence.[1]

When these preliminaries are completed the Worship may be begun. There are four introductory parts: the *basmalah*, i.e. saying, "In the name of Allah"; the *ta'awwudh*, the Seeking for Refuge; the *adhan* the Call; and the *iqamah*, the Institution. These are called the *shurut*, "stipulations," of the Worship. This term *shart* is also applied to the inner qualities or states of the heart, such as humbleness, magnifying, fear, awe, hope and shamefacedness, which, it is stipulated, with varying degrees of emphasis, are to accompany the outward acts and utterances of the Worship.

---

1. Al-Bajuri, *Commentary or Ibn Shujd'*, I, 157 f.

These *shurut,* Stipulations, of the Introduction are all performed by the worshipper in the Standing Position, which is the first of the *fara'id,* Prescribed, parts of the Worship. Another term also used by al-Ghazzali interchangeably with *faza'id* for the Prescribed Element is *arkan,* which is the term used most by his commentator. The word *fara'id* includes both the *arkan* and the *shurut,* but it is the outward acts and utterances which are the *arkan* that determine the validity of the Worship, rather than the *shurut,* the inner Stipulations. In this work al-Ghazzali includes the Intention among the Prescribed Elements, although in his *Wajiz* he places the Intention among the Stipulations.

The Prescribed Elements are those upon which the validity of the Worship normally depends. Modifications are allowed or required in certain performances of the Worship. For instance, the Standing Position is not an absolute requirement in the *nafl,* Supererogatory, Worship, nor the *fard,* Prescribed, Worship in the case of inability.

In addition to the Prescribed Elements there are *sunan,* Usage, acts the utterances in the Worship. They are of hardly less importance than the Prescribed Elements, for, while the Worship is valid, it is not complete without them. Some of these Usages are indeed so important that if they are omitted through forgetfulness they should have an extra prostration called *sajdat al-sahw,* Prostration of Forgetfulness or Oversight, to be performed before the Salutation, to make up for them. The four Usage Parts that should have the Prostration of Forgetfulness are called *ab'ad,* Parts.

Both the Prescribed Elements and the Usages include both *af'al,* Acts, and *adhkar.* Utterances, which are enumerated in the Text. Each one of these acts and utterances, of both the Elements and Usages, is done in certain recommended manners, which are called *adab,* Proprieties, and *hai'at,* Forms. The Standing is done with the head, hands and feet in specified positions. The *Takbir* is récited in a specified manner, with special care given to the vowelling of the consonants and with the utterance of the letters done while in certain positions.

The enumeration of the parts of the Worship is not fixed in Islam. The authors differ in the parts they consider to be separate elements, and consequently in the enumeration of the parts. Al-Ghazzali, for instance, considers the Bending down from the Standing Position until the worshipper comes to rest, with his palms on his knees and his back and head level, all as the Bowing, and counts it as one single Element. Others consider the Bending down to be the Bowing, and the *mutma'innah,* the Coming to Rest, in the bowing position to be a separate Element. Al-Ghazzali considers the Coming to Rest to be a Form of the Bowing, and only to that extent admits it to be a distinct part of the Worship. The situation is the same in the case of the Prostration.

Because of this variance in the differentiation of the parts of the Worship, some authors give the number of the Elements to be eleven, twelve, thirteen, up to eighteen and the case is similar with the *sunan,* Usages, of the Worship.

Another difficulty of enumeration arises through the fact that some authors count a part of the Worship only once in their list of the Elements or the Usages, although that same part will be repeated two or more times in the Worship. For instance, each *Rak'ah* of the Worship contains two Prostrations, but in the enumeration of the Elements they are counted as one, and similarly the Rising from the position of Prostration is counted as one Element.

A further development of this enumeration is that the parts are counted as if the Worship consisted of a single *Rak'ah,* Cycle, that is, as if it were a *Witr,* Odd, Worship of only one *Rak'ah,* although the five prescribed performances of the Worship have two, three or four *Rak'ahs,* with a consequently varying number of times of occurrence of each Element and with also a varying total number of Parts.

In the following table the Worship is analysed into the component parts, although not all the *ha'idt,* Forms, that al-Ghazzali mentions in connection with each Element or Usage are given.

Analytical Table of the Arkan, Elements, Sunan, Usages, and Hai'at, Forms, of the Worship

ARKAN				SUNAN			
af'al	*hai'at*	*adhkar*	*hai'at*	*af'al*	*hai'at*	*adhkar*	*hai'at*
Acts		Utterances					
1. Standing							
	Facing *qiblah*						
	Feet paired						
	Knees straight						
	Head lowered						
						2 Basmalah	
						3 Seeking Refuge	
						4 Call	
						5 Institution	
		6 Intention		7 Raising hands			
		8 *Takbir*			Palms out		
			Begins *alif*		Lowers hands		
			Ends ra'		Puts right on left		
					Two fingers extended		
					Others grasp writs		
						9 Opening Supplication	
						10 Seeking Refuge	
		11 Recites *al-Fatihah*					
			Perfects the letters			12 Says "*amin*"	
							Audibly
							Prolongs it
							Separates it from *al-Fatihah*
						13 Recites the *Surah*	

Analytical Table of the Arkan, Elements, Sunan, Usages, and Hai'at, Forms, of the Worship

ARKAN				SUNAN			
af'al	*hai'at*	*adhkar*	*hai'at*	*af'al*	*hai'at*	*adhkar*	*hai'at*
Acts		Utterances					Three verses Long in morning Short in evening
				14 Raises hands			15 *Takbir*
16 Bowing	Head and back level Hands on knees					17 *Tasbih*	Three, seven or ten times
18 Straightening	Stands briefly Stands long in morning			19 Raises hands		20 *Tasmi'* 21 *Takbir*	
22 Prostration	Knees on ground Hands on ground Forehead on ground Hands opposite shoulders					23 *Tasbih*	
24 Straightening	To sitting position As he raises head Sits on left foot Right foot is straight Hands on thighs Fingers extended					25 Says *Takbir* 26 Seven Supplications 27 *Takbir*	

28 Second Prostration
Like 22

Straightening (a component part of 1 *b* or 31)
Sitting briefly at close of each *rak'ah* not followed by Witnessing

1b Straightening
Standing, for Second *rak'ah*, with

1b Raising hands, etc.

34 Sitting for Last Witnessing
Left foot on ground

35 Last Witnessing
36 Blessing on Prophet
38 First Salutation
Turns to right
Cheeks seen from behind
Salutes angels and Muslims

29 *Tasbih*
Like 23

30 *Takbir*
Like 25

Or, instead of

31 Sitting for First witnessing
Sits on left foot
Folds right fingers
Extends index fingers

32 First Witnessing
33 Greeting and Blessing on Prophet

37 Supplication

39 Second Salutation
Turns to left

40 States Intention to stop.

The Kinds of the Worship

Passing from the consideration of the content of the Worship to the description of the kinds of the Worship, it is found that there are two divisions, the *fara'id,* Prescribed, and *nawafil,* Additional Supererogatory. It is noticed that the same word *fard* is used in connection with both the parts of a single performance of a Worship and with the Worship as a whole. Similarly, the word *sunnah,* Usage, is applied to some of the acts and utterances of the Worship, and to one of the kinds of the *nafl,* Supererogatory, Worship. The word *fard* is in common use among Muslim authors to mean the same performances that al-Ghazzali includes under that name. These are the five daily performances, consisting of the morning, noon, mid-afternoon, sunset and evening Worships. These are prescribed, required or obligatory. If they are abandoned intentionally, the penalty is death, or, among Hanafites, imprisonment until compliance.

The number of the *Rak'ahs*, Cycles, in the five daily performances of the Worship is fixed. The Morning Worship has two, Sunset has three, Noon, Mid-afternoon and Evening have four each. On Friday, the Congregational Worship takes the place of the Noon Worship, but if it is missed, the Noon Worship must be performed. The three performances of Noon, Afternoon and Evening may have two *Rak'ahs* each, instead of four, during a journey.

Al-Ghazzali calls all the performances of the Worship that are not Prescribed *nawafil,* Supererogatory, meaning "extra, additional". Other authors use other classifications, using the words *tatawwu'.* "voluntary", *wajib*, "behoving," *muwakkadah,* "confirmed," *mustahabb*, "liked," *mandub*, "recommended," *marghub fihi*, "desired," *sunnah,* "usage," *hasan*, "beautiful," *adab*, "proper," *fadilah,* "excellent," *hai'ah*, "form," and *nafl,* "additional". Al-Ghazzali has simply chosen certain of these words to label his classifications of the Worship, and states that there is no objection to the use of a different nomenclature on the parts of others. The important thing is to understand his use of the terms.

The *nafl*, Supererogatory, performances of the Worship then include all those that are not Prescribed. The religious law pronounces the doing of all these performances to be preferable to the omitting of them, and says that they secure reward, although the omitting of them is allowable, and not punished.

There are two concurrent classifications of them. The first classification relates to their excellence, and the second to the time of their occurrence.

Classified according to their excellence, the Supererogatory Worships are of three kinds, depending respectively upon the more or less consistent and constant performance of them by Muhammad, and upon the general excellence of performing Worship even when there is no definite example or special command of the Prophet to be followed.

The first of these classes is the *sunnah*, Usage or Customary, performances of the Worship. They are those that the Prophet usually performed and did not omit except for some cause. His consistent performance of them is known through traditions. Traditions of course vary in reliability, and that fact has bearing upon the question of the Prophet's continual performance of any specified Worship. For that reason the term *muwakkadah*, Strengthened, Confirmed, is also used by al-Ghazzali and others for these *sunnah* performances, sometimes instead of, and sometimes in addition to, the term *sunnah*. As in the case of the word *fard* the term *sunnah* is thus used to designate certain parts of each individual Worship and also a certain class of whole performances of the Worship.

The second class of the *nafl* Worship is the *mustahabb*, Liked. These are those that the Prophet performed sometimes and omitted sometimes, and which therefore it would be wrong to abandon entirely. To this class belong chiefly, although not entirely, the performance of the Worship by the individual alone, while the congregational performances are for the most part of the *muwakkadah*, Confirmed, class.

The third class is the *tatawwu'*, Voluntary, Worship. Concerning these there is no specific command or example of the Prophet except in traditions that are of weak authority. Their basis is rather the general principle that Worship is a good thing, and therefore, it is good to do as much of it as possible, and, further, one may show true zeal by performing voluntary Worship that he is not required or even definitely recommended to do.

The second classification is according to the time and the occasion of the performances of the *nafl* Worship. These are in four sub-divisions: the Daily, Weekly, Yearly and Occasional Performances, varying, as has been said, in their authority and excellence.

The first sub-division is the Daily performances. These, considered as to their time, are eight in number. Five of them consist of Worships of a varying number of *rak'ahs* Cycles, performed before or after, or both before and after, the regular Prescribed Worship. Al-Ghazzali uses the term *ratibah*, Fixed, Established in naming them, in connection with each of the five Prescribed performances. The object of an extra Worship immediately before or after the required Worship is, in the first case, to prepare one by preliminary practice to be in the right state of mind and body for the more important Worship to come; and in the second case, to make up, by the additional performance, for any possible defect or deficiency in the preceding Prescribed Worship.

The number of *rak'ahs* to be performed in these *ratibah* Worships is not certain, nor is it certain in the case of some of them, as, for instance, the Sunset *ratibah*, whether the particular Worship is to be performed before or after the Sunset Prescribed Worship. The uncertainty, in both instances, is, of course, due to conflicting traditions mentioning different numbers of *rak'ahs* and different times of performance for the same Worship.

In the case of the Noon *ratibah* six *rak'ahs* are recommended, four of them to be performed in a Worship before, and two in another Worship after the Prescribed performance. Furthermore, in this case, because there is a separate tradition mentioning two *rak'ahs* to be performed before the Prescribed Worship, it is said that two of the four *rak'ahs* in the *ratibah* Worship, before the *fard*, Prescribed, Noon Worship, are of the *muwakkadah*, Confirmed class, while the other two *rak'ahs* of the same performance remain simply *mustahabb*, Liked.

In addition to these five *ratibah*, Fixed, performances, connected with the five Prescribed performances, there are three other daily *nafl* Worships. There are the *witr*, Odd, Worship, the *duha*, Forenoon, Worship, and the *ihya'*, Enlivening, Worship.

The *witr,* Odd, Worship is a Worship of one, three, five or other odd number of *rak'ahs,* up to thirteen or even seventeen. It may be performed any time after the Sunset Worship up to the time for the morning Worship. It is preferably performed in connection with, or after, the *tahajjud,* Night, Worship, because there is a tradition that the *witr* is the last Worship of the night. Indeed, Al-Ghazzali says that it is this night Worship that is, Worship performed in the night after one has been asleep.

The *duha* Worship is a Confirmed Worship of four, six or eight *rak'ahs,* and, according to al-Bajuri, of from two to twelve *rak'ahs,* performed in the early, mid or late forenoon, according to different understanding of the word.

The third is the *ihya',* Enlivening, the cultivation or bringing into use, of the time between the two evening performances of the Worship, i.e. between the Sunset and the Evening Worships. Six is the number of *rak'ahs* al-Ghazzali quotes for it, and he classes it as Confirmed in excellence.

The second class after the Daily *nafl* Worship is the Weekly *nafl* Worship, i.e. Worship that is performed once each week. It is in two sub-divisions, the first containing Worship to be done in the daytime, and the second Worship to be done at night.

Al-Gazzali's treatment of this class is simply to repeat a tradition mentioning Worship on each day and night of the week. The traditions usually state the number of *rak'ahs* to be performed, the time they are to be done, and the particular reward attached to the Worship.

The third or Yearly class of *nafl* Worship includes four different performances, although the number of occasions exceeds that amount. The four are the two Feasts of *al-fitr,* the Breaking of the Fast of Ramadan, on the first day of Shawwal, the tenth month of the Muslim year, and of *al-adha,* the Sacrifice on the 10th of the month of Dhu al-Hijjah, the last of the Muslim year, at the conclusion of the Pilgrimage Ceremonies; the *tarawih,* Rest-giving, Worship of Ramadan; the Worship of Rajab, and the Worship of Sha'ban.

The Feast Worships are both of the Confirmed class in degree of excellence and have two *rak'ahs,* and are similarly performed, except as to time, for the first is delayed towards noon to allow for the distribution of alms, and the second is hastened so that the sacrifice may be slaughtered early. Both these performances are additional to the Daily Prescribed Worship and they differ from the ususal Worship in a number of particulars. For instance, except at Mecca, it is more excellent to perform this Worship outside the city, although on rainy days the usual congregational mosque is the preferred place. Further, the Worship of the Feasts differs from the regular Worships in that the usual *adhan,* Call, and *iqamah,* Institution, are not given. Al-Ghazzali prefers the phrase "The Worship is gathering!" as the Feast Call to Worship, while other authors add other phrases.

The *tarawih,* Rest-giving, Worship is so called because a brief rest is taken after every four *rak'ahs* which constitute a *tarwihah.* Each *tarwihah* consists of two complete Worships of two *rak'ahs* each, and five *tarwihahs* constitute the complete *tarawih* Worship. It is a Confirmed Worship, performed every night of Ramadan after the Evening Prescribed Worship. It is recommended to perform a complete recital of the Qur'an by reciting ten or more verses in each of the 580 or 600 *tarawih rak'ahs* performed in the twenty-nine or thirty days of that month.

Al-Ghazzali adds here a note to the effect that in the last half of the month it is liked that *witr,* Odd, Worship, performed, after the *tarawih,* Worship, should include the *qunut,* Supplication, a special petition recited in the Standing Position.

The Worship of Rajab occurs on the first Thursday of that month, the seventh of the Muslim year. It is a Worship of twelve *rak'ahs,* with special invocations. A fast is to be observed the whole day. The reward specified is forgiveness for all sins and the right of intercession for 700 relatives, for which reason it is also called *salat al-ragha'ib,* "Worship for which a large recompense is desired". The Worship is of the *mustahabb* class, and al-Ghazzali only adds it because the people of Jerusalem seemed to favour it. His commentator gives what purports to be an account of its origin, showing that it is a late addition to the performances of the Worship, and one that met much opposition.[2]

---

2. Sayyid Murtada, III, 422 f.

The Worship of Sha'ban occurs on the eve of the 15th of that month, the eighth of the Muslim year. It consists of fifty separate Worships of two *rak'ahs* each, or, as it is usually expressed, a hundred *rak'ahs* with fifty Salutations. It is of the *mustahabb* class, and sometimes was performed as a Congregational Worship. Because of the reward attached to its recital, consisting of the fulfilling of seventy needs with each of seventy glances of Allah at the Worshipper, the Worship is also called *salat al-khair*, the Good Worship.

In his fourth class of the *nafl*, Supererogatory, Worship, al-Ghazzali enumerates nine particulars, although in the rest of the *Ihya'* he mentions others belonging to this class. They are called Occasional Worships, because they are connected, not with specified times, but with particular occasions. Those that he enumerates are as follows.

The Worship of al-kusuf, *Eclipse of the Sun.* This is a Congregational Worship of two *rak'ahs*, differing from the usual *rak'ahs*, in that each contains two *ruku's*, Bowings, instead of one, as a special Shafi'ite feature. The Worship begins with the beginning of the eclipse and ends with its conclusion, and the first four long *surahs* are recommended to be recited.

The Worship of al-khusuf, *or Eclipse of the Moon.* This, among Shafi'ites, is similar to the former, except that the recital is to be done audibly instead of inaudibly. Both *kusuf* and *khusuf* are used of each luminary, although the more approved usage, and that of the astronomers, is that used by al-Ghazzali here.

These Worships are among those that may be performed in the Disliked times, although they are what al-Ghazzali calls less *muwakkadah* than the Feast Worships. Al-Bajuri calls them *masnun.*

The second is the Worship of the Request for Rain. It is a Congregational Worship, like that of the Feast, in that it is held outside the city, and has a similar Call to Worship, without the Institution formula. But it is unlike the Feast Worships in that poor clothes are to be worn, old people, children, women, and cattle are taken along. Jews and Christians subject to Muslim rule may also attend, according to al-Ghazzali, although al-Shafi'i considers that to be Disliked. The Worship is to be observed after a three-day fast has been proclaimed. Two *rak'ahs* are performed similar to those of the Feast Worship, except that, according to two texts, there are no *takbirs*, while the commentator emends and says that there is no difference. The underlying traditions differ. Another difference is that in this Worship the outer cloaks are to be worn upside down, the addresses have requests for forgiveness, in place of the *takbirs*, and in the second address the *imam* turns his back on the people. In turning the cloaks upside down, the right side is to be on the left, and the cloak is not to be inside out, although al-Ghazzali mentions that in the *Wajiz*,[3] forgetting that the right side cannot then be on the left.

The Funeral Worship, more properly, the Worship connected with the death of a person, differs from all the other performances of Worship in that it does not contain any *rak'ah*. It is for that reason the *salat al-janazah*, or *jinazah*, is used in grammars to illustrate the *idafat al-naqisah*, "the incomplete connection" because its subject-matter is not complete. The word *janazah* is applied to both the dead person and the bier on which he is placed. The Worship is performed for all Muslims, except the *shahid*, "martyr," killed in the course of battle with unbelievers. When Muslims and unbelievers are indistinguishable among the dead in battle all are to be buried, and the Muslims are to be singled out in the Worship.

The Funeral Worship is of the *fard kifayah* class, i.e. the requirement for its performance is satisfied when one or more of the Muslims take it upon themselves to fulfil it as a duty.[4] It has, according to al-Ghazzali, seven essential Elements, consisting of (1) statement of Intention; (2) the Standing Posture; (3) four *takbirs*, or possibly five. After the first comes (4) the Fatihah; (5) the Blessing upon the Prophet after the second *takbir;* (6) the Supplication for the dead after the third *takbir*, and (7) the Salutation.

Besides this Worship there is a Greeting bestowed upon the dead people of the cemetery when the company arrives there, and another Supplication offered when the body is lowered into the grave.

The fourth is the Worship of the Greeting of the Mosque.

---

3. I, 44.
4. Ibid., I, 47 A.

It is a Confirmed Usage and is performed upon entering the mosque even if that happens to be when the *imam* is lecturing, although it should not then be a separate, distinct Worship of its own, but may be Prescribed or Substitution Worship due from him. Its object is to occupy with Worship the beginning of the time one enters the mosque. It may, therefore, be performed in the five Disliked times for Worship.

The fifth is the Worship after the Ablution. It consists of two *rak'ahs and is of the mustahabb,* Liked, class. Al-Ghazzali states that the Intention is to be omitted from this Worship while al-Nawawi says that it may be made.

The sixth is the Worship of two *rak'ahs* to be performed upon Entering or Leaving the House. Under this head come all the performances of Worship that are recommended to be performed upon the beginning of each occurrence of importance, such as the wearing of the *ihram* when nearing Mecca for the Pilgrimage, and the beginning to the *tawaf*, or Encircling, of the Ka'bah while on Pilgrimage, and upon starting and returning from a journey. The invocation of "In the name of Allah", uttered upon eating and drinking, comes under this sub-division, for it may be extended to become a full performance of the Worship. Likewise the marriage contract, and the giving of advice, may be prefaced with the *basmalah,* and Invocations of Praise and Blessing upon the Prophet. The most important events, such as journeys, are recommended to have two full *rak'ahs.*

Under this sub-division may be mentioned also the modifications of the *nafl*, Supererogatory, Worship allowed to one on a long journey, for these may be performed walking and riding upon an animal or a ship. The traveller faces the *qiblah* only when stating the Intention, and he nods his head for the Bowing and the Prostration. Al-Murtada says that unless it is easy even the facing of the *qiblah* is not obligatory.[5]

The seventh is the Worship of the Request for Prospering. It is a Worship of two *rak'ahs.* When it is finished the matter of anxiety is named and then the Supplication, which is the request for the blessing, prospering and favour of Allah, is presented with

---

5. VI, 435 f.

uplifted hands in the traditional words as given in the Text. When this has been done the man goes away to that for which his bosom becomes dilated, i.e. to that which is made to seem acceptable to him.[6] The Request for Prospering is to be offered for any matter of concern. Sayyid Murtada records that he made the request for prospering in the matter of giving his commentary on the *Ihya'* the name of the "Gift of the God fearing Masters".[7] Corruptions of this Worship and Supplication, consisting of the casting of lots and chance opening of the Qur'an and other books and magic, are strongly condemned in Sunni Islam.

The eighth is the Worship of Need. It is a Worship of twelve *rak'ahs* with specified Recitals and is followed by the Supplication of Need, offered in the attitude of Prostration. The need may be any pressing necessity, religious or worldly. The text of the request includes the phrase "I ask Thee by Thy greatest Name" which has found so large a place in magic in Islam. It is recommended that this Supplication should not be taught to the foolish, lest they encourage one another in antinomianism.

The ninth is the Worship of Praise. This is a special Worship unconnected with any set time or circumstance. It has four *rak'ahs* with specified Recitals in them, and specified Invocations during each of the four attitudes in each *rak'ah,* so that the same Invocation is repeated three hundred times during the Worship.

This is the last of the performances of the Worship mentioned by al-Ghazzali in the Book of the Mysteries of the Worship. In addition to them three modifications of the Prescribed Worship are recommended, and three special Prostrations are prescribed or recommended.

The first of the modifications of the Prescribed Worship is that allowed to the traveller, for he may perform two instead of four *rak'ahs* in the Noon. Afternoon and Evening Worships, performing the Morning and Sunset Worships as usual.

The second modification is that the uniting of the Noon with the Afternoon, and the Sunset with the Evening Worship is

6. Cf. Qur'an, xcv:—8.
7. Sayyid Murtada I, 3, I, 11.

allowable, for the traveller and for the one accustomed to Worship with the congregation, when it is raining. The Noon Worship would be performed before the Afternoon, and separated from it only by the length of time it takes for the *iqamah*, Institution, of the Worship.

The third is the Worship of Fear, that is, of the one who is in fear. The Qur'anic basis is iv. 103. It is, according to al-Bajuri,[8] of sixteen varieties, of which al-Ghazzali mentions four in his *Wajiz*,[9] and in his *Ihya'*.

The variations are according to the stress of danger and the number and position of the enemy. In the circumstances of utmost fear, it is impossible to leave the battle when the time for the Prescribed Worship comes, the Worship may be performed on foot on riding, with or without facing the *qiblah*, with nodding of the head in the place of the Bowing and the Prostration, with the guarding against crying out and giving unnecessary blows.

This Worship may also be performed by one fleeing from fire, drowning and ferocious beast, just as it is permissible to wear silk, or the skin of a dog or pig, in case of sudden fear.

The special Prostrations, which may be considered as partial Worships, are the *sajdat* or *sujud al-sahw*, the Prostration of Forgetfulness, and the *sajdat al-tilawah*, Prostration of the Recital of the Qur'an, and the *sajdat al-shukr*, the Prostration of Thanksgiving.

The Prostration of Recital is required to be performed when, in the course of the reading, i.e. reciting of the Qur'an, the Muslims reaches one of the fourteen Verses of Prostration. These verses are given in a note to the Text.[10] This Prostration has the same preliminary requirements as the usual Worship. The least Prostration is simply placing the forehead on the ground, while the most complete includes the Standing Posture and a *takbir* with the Raising of the hands; then a *takbir* while going down for the Prostration, and then a Supplication appropriate to the portion

8. I, 288.
9. I, 40 f.
10. Note 34, p. 12.

just read, followed by a *takbir* on rising. and then the Salutation. Sayyid Murtada says *al-tali*, "the reciter," is a *musalli*, "worshipper," that is a *munaji*, "one who is communing" with Allah.[11]

In the *Wajiz*, al-Ghazzali states that this Prostration is incumbent upon both the *imam* who is reciting and the hearer of the verse.[12]

The Prostration of Forgetfulness or Oversight is a *sunnah*, Usage, that may or may not be performed whenever any of the four *ab'ad*, Parts, of the *sunnah*, Usage, items of the Worship are unintentionally omitted. These are the First Witnessing, the *qunut*, the Blessing upon the Messenger of Allah in the First Witnessing and the Blessing on his family in the Last Witnessing. It is performed at any of six places before the Salutation.

Any of the other *sunan*, Usages, of the Worship, according to al-Ghazzali, may be made up by a Prostration,[13] although al-Bajuri, calling these other *sunan*, Usages, by the name of *hai'at*, Forms, says they are not.[14]

If the *arkan*, Prescribed Elements, of the Worship are unintentionally omitted they are repeated. This is called *tadaruk*, "supplying," what was omitted through inadvertence.[15]

Any *rukn*, Element, if omitted, is to be performed before engaging in the next Element; otherwise, either the Worship is invalid, or he supplies the omission and performs the rest of the Worship over again, together with an Oversight Prostration.[16]

The Prostration of Thanksgiving is a *sunnah*, Usage, performed on the occasion of the receipt of some unusual favour, or the warding off of some misfortune. It is liked to be performed also before an evil person out of thankfulness for the warding off of disobedience and as a warning to him[17]. The Second Book

---

11. IV, 485 D.
12. I, 32.
13. *Al-Wajiz*, I, 30.
14. op, cit., I, 200.
15. *Al-Wajiz*, I, 30.
16. Al-Bajuri, op. cit., I, 224 f.
17. *Al-Wajiz*, I, 32.

of the Fourth Quarter of the *Ihya'* deals with the subjects of Patience and Thanksgiving.

Other Expressions of the Devotional Life

Except for the Prostration of the Recital of the Qur'an and of Thanksgiving, all the preceding forms of devotion consisted of the particular ceremony called the Worship, comprising special elements and known utterances, accompanied by certain stipulations, restricted within specified times,[18] or else of modifications of that ceremony. The two exceptions above mentioned consist in parts of that ceremony and are included by al-Ghazzali in his treatment of the Worship in his book on *Fiqh*, called *al-Wajiz.*

Of the recommended and voluntary methods of *ibadah*, "religious service," paid by the tongue, to use al-Ghazzali's phrase, the first in importance is *al-tildwah*, the Recital of the Qur'an. It is the subject of Book viii of the First Quarter of the *Ihya'*.

He presents first the excellence of the Qur'an and the recital of it. Then he describes the proper method of its outward recital, which includes ten items, some of which are as follows: (1) The reader should be ceremonially clean and should stand or sit sedately, although the last two points are not absolutely required. (2) The amount recited may vary. Some have finished the Qur'an twice in a day and night, and others once a month. (3) The Qur'an is usually divided into seven sections, although divisions into five, ten, thirty, and other numbers of parts, are mentioned or allowed. (4) The recital should be prefaced by the Seeking Refuge formula. (5) The rites of the Verses of Prostration should be observed. (6) The recital should be at least loud enough for the reciter himself to hear.

There are ten inward acts of the heart and understanding that accompany the recital, such as causing the heart to be present, and the understanding to appreciate what is read, and for the reciter to attend as if he were hearing speech from Allah and not from himself.

Next in importance to the Recital of the Qur'an, according to al-Ghazzali, is the *dhikr*, Invocation. He devotes Book ix of the

18. Jurjani, *Ta'rifat*, p. 139.

First Quarter of the *Ihya'* to the consideration of *al-adhkar* and *al-da'awat*, Invocations and Supplications. He presents first the evidence of the excellence of the Invocations and the gathering for reciting them from the Qur'an Traditions and Records, Then he shows the excellence of the various invocations, such as *al-tahlil*, "There is no god but Allah," with several additional phrases; *al-tasbih*, "O the Praise of Allah"; *al-tahmid*, "The praise or thanksgiving belongs to Allah". The names of Allah are also used. The number of repetitions of these and other phrases and the amount of reward the repetitions bring are both recorded.

The reason for the superiority of the *dhikr* over the forms of religious service involving hardship can be revealed only by the "unveiled knowledge," he says but this much may be mentioned that the beneficial effect is the constant remembrance of Allah, along with the presence of the heart.

The *du'a'*, Supplication, is another of the methods of communion with Allah. It includes the asking for forgiveness and the blessing upon the Prophet as well as request for needs. Al-Ghazzali mentions ten proprieties that are to be observed in offering supplications, among which are the observance of the Day of 'Arafah in the Pilgrimage ceremonies, the month of Ramadan and Friday of every week: the offering of Supplications after the Prescribed Worship, when fasting, when facing the *qiblah*, repeating the request at three times, meanwhile being hopeful of an affirmative reply and repentant towards Allah.

Al-Ghazzali gives three chapters of Traditional Supplications the prayers of the Muslim saints--for all times and occasions. Then he discusses the value of Supplications in view of the immutability of predestination. His answer is that the Supplication for the Warding Off of Evil and the Bringing of Mercy is among the things predestined. He Who decreed the good decreed it by a cause, and He Who decreed the evil decreed its being warded off by a cause. Further, supplication is the marrow of religious service, and it requires the presence of the heart with Allah.

The Tenth Book of the First Quarter of the *Ihya'* is the *Kitab Tartib al-Awrad.* Al-Ghazzali uses the word *wird* as a "portion" of the day and night. He divides the day into seven *wirds*: one between dawn and sunrise; two each between sunrise and noon,

noon, and *'asr*, "mid-afternoon," *'asr*, and sunset. The night has, including the period of sleep, five *wirds*, two before and two after the sleep *wird*. These times are to be occupied by the four devotional exercises: Invocation, Supplication, Recital of the Qur'an and Meditation. The last he discusses in Book ix of the Fourth Quarter of the *Ihya'*. His object in the *Book of Wirds*, Portions, is simply to set forth the manner of the previously mentioned Supplications and the method of spending the day and night in pious occupation. *Wird* then means the portion of time used in devotional recitation, or the devotional recitations themselves, including portions of the Qur'an, devotional phrases, and, nowadays, also commentaries on the Qur'an.

A word of similar meaning to *wird* is *hizb*. It is that recital of the Qur'an or performance of the Worship which a man imposes on himself. So, in the *Taj al-'Arus*, I, 208. This is a development of the original meaning of the word, which is "party," "division". It was early applied to divisions of the Qur'an. The darwish fraternities applied the term of their special services. Then special supplications, prepared by individuals, were used as *hizbs*, so that now *ahzab* for the days of the week are in common use.

The *hirz*, "protection," is a petition for protection and refuge and is simply a *du'a'*, "supplication," of a special character. Similarly, the *istignathah*, "cry for help," is a petition for aid and succour. The term *waza'if*, "offices," "duties," is also used to cover the directions and recitals for spending set times at Worship.

There are still other forms of expression of devotion that need only brief mention. These are the Poems of Petition, which are a kind of hymns of Allah's praise, and also the declarations of the praise of Allah, and descriptions of His qualities, usually in *saj'*, "rhymed prose," at the beginning of books.

Additional to these methods of expressing devotion, it is necessary to note several other general customs. The first is the *mawlid*, "birthday anniversary". There is a large and increasing *mawlid* literature of petitions and poems of praise for the celebration of the birthday anniversaries of Muhammad and noted saints of Islam.

The second is the *i'tikaf* "retreat" within a mosque, for a day, preferably Friday, or longer, in order to spend the time between the Prescribed Worships in quiet performances of the *nafl* Worship and the four other devotional exercises. The last third of Ramadan is a favourite time for the Retreat.

Another is the *ziyarah*, "visit," to some special place usually the tomb of a saint, for the offering of the Worship, supplications and invocations, in the name of the saint.

This concludes the survey of the devotional exercises of the Muslims and indicates the paramount importance of the ceremony of the Worship in all private and public religious service.

Contents

Contents

Introduction

In the Name of Allah, the Merciful and Compassionate One

Praise belongs to Allah, Who overwhelms His creatures with His favours, and fills their hearts with the lights and duties of religion, whose descent[1] from the throne of majesty to the nearest heaven[2] is, of the degrees of mercy, one of His kindnesses.[3] He differs from kings, for all His unique majesty and grandeur, in inspiring His creation to ask and supplicate, for He says:[4] "Is there any who supplicates? I will answer him!" and, "Is there any who asks forgiveness? I will forgive him!" He differs from sultans in opening the door and lifting the veil, and permitting His creatures confidential communion, by the performances of Worship, however their circumstances may change, whether in congregations or solitary places. Moreover, He does not limit Himself to permission, but rather shows favour and kindness by inspiring desire and by calling. Any other than He is of the weak kings, who do not freely grant private audience, except after the presentation of a gift or a bribe. So-O His praise! How great is His state, and strong His authority and complete His kindness and general His beneficence!

---

1. The descent of Allah from the highest heaven to that nearest earth takes place in the last third of the night. The tradition in part of the one immediately following. It is an encouragement to the *tahajjud*, Night Worship, one of the most excellent of the acts of religious service, The descent is not to be understood literally.
2. The allusion here is probably to Qur'an, lxv. 12.
3. The allusion may be to the following tradition of Abu Hurairah's, wherein the same word is used for "kindness": Allah has one hundred mercies; of them He has sent down one among mankind and jinn, cattle and serpents, in which and by which they are kind to one another and by which the wild beast is kind to its offspring. He reserved ninety-nine mercies by which He will be merciful to His creatures on Resurrection Day" (*Mishkat al-Masabih*, Cairo, 1309, Vol. III, Bk. X, Chap. IV, Division 1).
4. This tradition has Qur'anic basis in xl, 62.

May blessing and peace indeed be upon Muhammad, His elected Prophet and His chosen intimate, and upon his family and his Companions, keys of guidance and lamps in darkness!

"Worship is the support of the religion" and the handle[5] of certainty, the chief of good works, and the most conspicuous of the acts of obedience. In the department of canon law, we have investigated,[6] in *Basit al-Madhhab*,[7] "The Wide Way", *Al-Wasit,* "The Medium", and *Al-Wajiz,* "The Brief", the Worship's trunks and branches, expending abundance of care upon its rare ramifications and exceptional occurrences, that they may be a treasure-store for the *mufti,* canon lawyer, from which he may seek help, and may be something reliable for him, to which he may flee for aid and refer.

We now, in this book, limit ourself to what the devotee must needs have of canon law, consisting of the Worship's external acts and its inner mysteries, while revealing refinements of the inner qualities hidden in the qualities of humbleness, singleness of devotion and intention which it has not been customary to mention in the department of canon law.

We are arranging the book in seven chapters: 1. The Excellences of the Performances[8] of the Worship; 2. The Particulars of the External Acts of the Worship; 3. The Particulars[9] of the Inward Acts Thereof; 4. The Leadership by the *Imam* and the Iimitation (by the Worshipper); 5. The Friday Worship and Its *Adab,* Proprieties; 6. The Various Problems from which Trouble Commonly Arises, and which the Devotee Needs to Know; 7. The Voluntary Performances of the Worship, etc.

---

5. The "handle" is the strap by which the water-skin is carried about, and the "certainty" is vision face to face by the power of faith, not by argument and proof; so comments Sayyid Murtada, *Ithaf al-Sadat al-Mutlaqin.*
6. These works are mentioned in Sayyid Murtada, op. cit., I, 41-43, giving a list of al-Ghazzali's books.
7. Al-Ghazzali was a Shafi'i.
8. This translation is from the text in Sayyid Murtada (op. cit.) Other texts have *salah,* singular instead of plural.
9. *Tafdil* in the text of the *Ihya'* published by Dar al-Kutub al'Arbiyat al-Kubra, Cairo, 1334, instead of *tafsil,* as here.

1

The Excellences of the Worship, Prostration, Congregation, Call to Worship, Etc.

The Excellence of the Call to Worship

He (may Allah bless him and give him peace[10]) said, "Three there will be on Resurrection Day upon a hill of black musk whom no accounting will frighten and whom no fear will reach, until there is surcease from what is (happening) among men: (1) a man who recited the Qur'an, out of desire for the Face[11] of Allah (Who is almighty and exalted), and led (in Worship) a people well-pleased with him; (2) a man who gave the Call[12] to Worship in a mosque and summoned to Allah, out of desire for the Face of Allah; and (3) a man who was tested by slavery[13] in this life,[14]

---

10. The eulogia will be translated once upon their first occurrence.
11. For al-Ghazzali's explanation of the word "face," as applied to man, and meaning "the self," or, more closely, "the consciousness," see below, Chapter 3: "Inward Stipulations" (Murtada, op. cit., I, 142), Sayyid Murtada says, 'face" means "the essence of the man" and "the whole of his body" (p. 104A). The meaning of "the Face of Allah" belongs to "the unveiled knowledge" (ibid., I, 164).
12. Sayyid Murtada (op. cit.) adds that the noun *adhan* is from adhana, "to inform," and then was applied to a particular giving of information at a particular time, His treatment of it is at p. 132. He says it is a *sunnah kifayah* for the congregation, i.e. a Usage fulfilled if some perform it, and a *sunnah* 'ain for the individual worshipping alone, i.e. he may do it himself, or omit it.
13. Sayyid Murtada reads *riqq,* "slavery," instead of *rizq,* "apportioned provision," which the other texts have, to make the tradition accord with the other versions of it which he quotes.
14. *Al-dunya* is used in the Qur'an alone or with *al-haia,* as "the nearer life," and consequently "this world" and is contrasted with *al-akhirah,*

but that did not make him too busy for the work of the next life."

Muhammad said, "No *jinni*, or man, or thing hears the Call of the *mu'adhdhin* but he will bear witness for him on Resurrection Day." Muhammad said, "The hand of the Compassionate One is upon the head of the *mu'adhdhin until* he finishes his Call." It is said in exposition of the saying of Allah, "And who speaks better words than he who summons to Allah and does what is right?" (Qur'an xli. 33) that it was sent down concerning the *mu'adhdhins.* Muhammad said, "Whenever you hear the Call, say the like of that which the *mu'adhdhin* says"; and that is desirable[15] except when he gives the *hai'alatain* (i.e., "Come for Worship! Come for prosperity") for in their case he says, "There is no power or strength but in Allah!" And when he says, "The time for Worship has come!" he says, "May Allah institute it and may He continue it as long as the heavens and the earth continue!" At the *tathwib,*[16] what he says is, "You have spoken the truth, you have acted rightly, you have given good advice!" And at the finish he says, "O Allah, Lord of this complete Call and instituted Worship, give Muhammad mediation and excellence and raise him up to the praise-worthy station which Thou didst promise him: 'Thou dost not break a promise!" (Qur'an, iii. 192). Sa'id b. al-Musayyab[17] said, "Whoever worships in a desert place has an angel worship

---

used alone or with *al-dar,* as "the other, or last, abode," hence, "the next world".

15. *Mahbub* is used in a technical sense, and is Sayyid Murtada's synonym for *mustahabb,* found in the other texts. It is applied to something for the doing of which there is reward, without any blame for the occasional omission of it.

16. Lane, *Lexicon,* gives (p. 361) five uses of *tathwib;* calling to worship and other things; repeated call; a special phrase in the call of the *mu'adhdhin* (a) "Prayer! May Allah have mercy on you! Prayer!" (b) "Prayer is better than sleep!" the chanting of the *iqdmah* by those who arrive on time; supererogatory prayer. Al-Ghazzali uses it here as the special phrase "The Worship is better than sleep" in the morning Call to the Worship.

17. Abu al-Qasim Sa'id b. al-Musayyab (he himself preferred Musayyib), the chief of the first series of Successors, and son-in-law of Abu Hurairah; 15 or 16-91 or 95 A.H. [Sayyid Murtada says 94 (I, 116 D)].

on his right and an angel worship on his left, but, if he gives the Call and the *iqamah,* Institution, there worship behind him the likenessess of mountains consisting of angels."

The Excellence of the Prescribed Worship

Allah (Who is exalted in and of Himself) said, "The Worship was prescribed and timed for the believers (Qur'an, iv. 104).

Muhammad has said, "Five performances of the Worship has Allah prescribed upon His creatures. So, whoever brings them, and does not miss anything of them by slighting their right, has a compact with Allah that He will make him enter the Garden. And whoever does not bring them does not have a compact with Allah: if He will, He will punish him, or if He will, He will make him enter the Garden."

Muhammad said, "The five performances of the Worship are like a river, fresh and deep, beside the door of any of you, into which he plunges five times every day, and what do you think that leaves of his uncleanness?" They replied, "Not anything!" He said, "So the five performances of the Worship remove offences as water removes dirt."

Muhammad said, "The performances of the Worship are an atonement for whatever small sins occur between them, so long as you have avoided the great."[18]

Muhammad said, "Between us and the hypocrites[19] there is the attendance of the Night and of the Morning (Worships), which they are not able to do."

Muhammad said, "Whoever meets Allah as a misser of the Worship (will find that) Allah will not pay attention to any part of his good works."

Muhammad said, "The Worship is the support of the religion,

---

18. A "great" sin is something clearly prohibited, for which punishment, in this life and the next, is clearly laid down in the religious law.
19. One who testifies and works but does not believe is a hypocrite, *munafiq;* one who testifies and does not work, but believes, is a transgressor, *fasiq;* one who stops short with testifying is an unbeliever, *kafir.* For the historical Hypocrites or disaffected of Medina, see the lives of Muhammad and commentaries on the Qur'an, lxiii.

so whoever abandons it has thrown over the religion."

Muhammad was asked, "Which of the works is most excellent?" He replied, "The Worship at its appointed times."

Muhammad said, "Whoever perseveres in the fire (Worships) along with complete observance of their purification and their times, will have light, and, on Resurrection Day, proof. Whoever misses them will be assembled with Pharaoh and Haman."

Muhammad said, "The key of the Garden is the Worship."

He said, "Allah has not prescribed upon His creatures, after the confession of the unity, anything more beloved to Him than the Worship. If there were anything more beloved to Him than it, His angels would devote themselves by means of it, but some of them bow, some of them prostrate, and some stand and sit."

The Prophet said, "Whoever abandons the Worship intentionally has become a *kafir,* unbeliever," that, is one near to being removed from the faith by the loosening of its handle and the falling of its support, as it is said of one who draws near to a village,[20] "he has reached it and entered it".

He also said, "Whoever abandons the Worship intentionally has become free of the protection of Muhammad."

Abu Hurairah[21] (Allah be pleased with him) said, "Whoever performs the ablution, but does his ablution well, and then goes out, making for the Worship, is in worship as long as he is making for the Worship, and there is written for him with one of his footsteps one good work, and there is erased for him with the other one evil deed. So, whenever one of you hears the *iqamah,* Institution, it is not fitting for him to hang back, for the one of you who gets the greatest reward is the one whose house is the

---

20. This is a favourite illustration, used in opposite senses, to avoid as undesirable situation. It is quoted in the *Lisan al-'Arab,* IV, 472, to show the *al-wurud,* "coming to" or "into" is not *al-dukhul,* "entrance," in explanation of Qur'an, xix, 72, "There is not any of you but is coming to it." i.e. the Fire.
21. Abu Hurairah, "the father of Little Cat," was a Companion and the most prolific traditionist, as well as sometime governor of al-Bahrain. He died in 75 or 58 A.H.

most distant." They asked, "Why, O Abu Hurairah?" He replied "On account of the large number of the footstep."

It is related that the first of the works of the creature that is looked into Resurrection Day is the Worship. Then, if it is found to be complete, it is accepted from him, along with the rest of his work. If it is found to be deficient, it is returned to him, along with the rest of his work.

Muhammad said, "O Abu Hurairah! enjoin the Worship upon your family, for Allah will bring you provision[22] from a place you do not reckon upon."

One of the learned said, "One who worships is like a merchant to whom no profit results until his capital is secure, and likewise no *nafilah*,[23] Supererogatory, Worship is accepted for the one who worships until he makes a proper payment[24] of the Prescribed Worship."

---

22. *Rizq* is the apportioned provision or allowance which Allah creates and supplies to all His creatures, for their bodies and minds (*Lisan al-'Arab*, XI, 405).
23. Al-Ghazzali divides all the performances of the Worship into two classes: *fard*, Prescribed, and *nafl*, Additional, Supererogatory. The latter class has three sub-divisions: *sunnah*, Usage, or *mu'akkadah*, Confirmed, *mustahabb*, Liked, and *tatawwu'*, Voluntary.
24. *Al-ada'* is the payment of an obligation itself at its divinely enjoined time. The term may be applied to both Prescribed and Supererogatory acts which have times appointed by the Divine law, when those acts are performed within, but not before or after, their time limits. It is of three classes: (1) The "perfect," *kamil*, Payment, such as is performed by the *imam* and one who is on hand in the mosque for all the Worship. (2) A "defective," *naqis*, payment is, for instance, a Worship performed by one who worships alone, or who arrives at the mosque somewhat late. (3) Payment "resembling the substitution performance," *skibh al-qada'*, is performed by one who arrives after the *imam* finishes, because, in respect of the time, it is an *ada'*, but in respect of the fact that he was under obligation to perform the worship along with the *imam*, it is *qada'*. Further, it is distinguished from *al-i'adah*, "the repetition" of the performance within the appointed time, by being called the "first" performance. The i'adah is required, when, for some reason, the first performance is defective (Jurjani, *Ta'rifat*, p. 14).

Abu Bakr[25] used to say, "Whenever the Worship time comes, stand up to the fire which you have ignited, and put it out!"

The Excellence of Performing Completely the Essential Elements[26]

Muhammad said, "The Prescribed Worship is like a balance: whoever pays is repaid in full."

Yazid al-Raqashi[27] said, "The Worship of the Messenger of Allah was symmetrical, as though it were measured in a balance."

Muhammad said, "Two men of my people will perform the Worship and their bowing and their prostration will be one (the same), but between their two Worships there will be what there is between heaven and earth." He referred to humbleness (towards Allah).

He said, "On Resurrection Day, Allah will not look at the creature who does not straighten up his backbone between his bowing and his prostration."

He also said, "Does he, who turns his face round in the Worship, not fear that Allah will turn his face into the face of a donkey?"

He said, "Whoever performs the Worship for its appointed time and does its ablution and performs completely its bowing, its prostration and its humbleness (for him) it ascends, white and shining, saying 'May Allah keep you as you have kept me!' And whoever performs the Worship for its unappointed time, and does not do its ablution, and does not perform completely its bowing, its prostration and its humbleness, (for him) it ascends, black and dark, saying, 'May Allah neglect you as you have neglected me!" until, when it is in the place where Allah wills it to be, it is folded up as a shabby garment is folded up, and his face is

25. Abu Bakr al-Siddiq, the first khalifah (d. 13 A.H.). He received the surname of "the Very Veracious" on account of his asserting the truth of the Prophet's miraculous night-journey. *Al-Sidaiq* is used of a man who is truthful in his speech and belief, and who has verified his truthfulness by his act (Raghib, *Mufradat al-Qur'an,* p. 278).
26. Al-Ghazzali divides the component parts of the Worship into *fard'id,* Prescribed Elements, *sunan,* Usage, Customary, Parts, *adab,* proprieties, and *hai'dt,* Forms (Sayyid Murtada, op. cit., I, 99).
27. Yazid b. Abau al-Raqashi, pious traditionist.

struck with it."

He also said, "The most evil of mankind, as regards stealing, is the one who steals from his Worship."

Ibn Mas'ud[28] and Sal'man[29] said. "The Worship is a measure: so, whoever gives full measure is fully repaid, and whoever gives light measure--well, he knows what Allah said about those giving light measure!" (Qur'an, lxxxiii. 1).

The Excellence of the Congregational Worship

Muhammad said, "Worship in the congregation is more excellent than Worship alone by twenty-seven degrees."

Abu Hurairah relates that Muhammad missed some men at the Worship. So he said, "I surely was anxious to order a man to conduct the Worship with the people, and then (myself) to turn away after men who remain away from it, and burn up their houses for them!"

In another narrative (it is said), "Then I would go after the men who remain away from it and give orders about them, so that their houses should be burnt for them by means of a bundle or firewood. If any of them knew that he would find a fat bone, or two trotters,[30] he would be present at it," meaning the evening Worship.

'Uthman[31] has reported a *marfu'*[32] statement of the Prophet's: "Whoever is present at the evening Worship, it is indeed (for him)

---

28. 'Abdallah b. Mas'ud b. Ghafil, a Companion of the Prophet (d. 32 or 33 A.H.).
29. 'Abu 'Abdallah Salman al-Farisi al-Khair, *mawla,* manumitted slave," of the Messenger of Allah (d. 34, 35, or 36 A.H..).
30. The treatment of *mirmah,* sometimes, *marmah,* is fuller in the Lisdn *al-'Arab,* XIX, 53 f, than in al-Murtada's *Taj al-'Arus,* X, 156. About ten meanings are listed, centred around "arrows," "hoofs, "and "trotters," of which the last seems to fit the context best. The tradition is in al-Bukhari, *Sahih, Kitab al-Ahkam,* ed. with commentary of al-Qastallani, II, 25. The word is used in the plural in the sense of "thunderbolts" in Baidawi on the Qur'an, xvii, 38.
31. Abu 'Amr 'Uthman, b. 'Affan, the third khalifah (d. 35 A.H.).
32. A *marfu'* tradition is a statement from the Messenger of Allah, reported by a Companion (Jurjani, op. cit., p. 224).

as if he stood half a night (in Worship); and whoever is present at the morning Worship, (for him) it is as if he indeed stood a night."

Muhammad said, "Whoever performs a Worship in congregation has filled his chest with Divine service."

Sa'id b. al-Musayyab said, "The *mu'adhdhin* has not given the Call of Worship for twenty years except while I was in the mosque."

Muhammad b. Wasi'[33] said, "I desire only three things from this life: a brother who, if I become crooked, will straighten me; some sustenance from the apportioned provision that is lawful and needs no claim, and Worship in congregation, in which forgetfulness is removed from me, and the reward of which is recorded for me" (cf. Qur'an, lxxxii. 10-12).

It is related that Abu 'Ubaidah b. al-Jarrah[34] was *imam* (leader in Worship) for a people on one occasion, and when he departed he said, "Satan kept at me just now until I thought I had superiority over anyone else: I will never act as *iman* again!"

Al-Hasan[35] said, "Do not worship behind a man who does not follow the learned!"

Al-Nakha'i[36] said, "The one who acts as *imam* for men, without knowledge, is like the one who measures the water in the sea--he does not know its increase from its decrease."

Hatim and Deaf[37] said, "The Worship in the congregation escaped me, and Abu Ishaq al-Bukhari[38] alone condoled with me.

---

33. Muhammad b. Wasi'al-Azdi al-Basri (d. 120 A.H. Sayyid Murtada here says 127 A.H.).
34. Abu 'Ubaidah b. al-Jarrah (d. 18 A.H.).
35. Abu Sa'id al-Hasan b. Abi al-Hasan Yasar al-Basri, prominent and learned traditionist (d. 110 A.H.).
36. When the *nisbah* "al-Nakha'i," is used alone, says Sayyid Murtada here, it usually refers to Abu 'Imran and 'Ammar Ibrahim b. Yazid b. al-Aswad b. 'Amr b. Rabi' b. Harithah b. Sa'd b. Malik b. al-Nakha'i, jurisprudent (d 95-96 A.H.), or the reference may be to Ibrahim's maternal uncle, al-Aswad b. Yazid, also a jurisconsult (d. 75A.H.).
37. Abu "Abd al-Rahman Hatim b. 'Alwan (or 'Anwan) the Deaf, ascetic.
38. Abu Ishaq Ibrahim b. Isma'il al-Saffar al-Bukhari (not the author of the *Sahih*) (d. 534 A.H.).

But, had a child of mine died, more than ten thousand would have condoled with me, for religious misfortune is lighter with men than this life's misfortune."

Ibn 'Abbas[39] (may Allah be pleased with both 'Abbas and his son!) said, "Whoever hears the Call and does not respond does not mean good and good is not meant for him."

Abu Hurairah said, "Truly, that the ear of a son of Adam should be filled with molten lead would be better than that he should hear the Call and then not respond!"

It is related that Maimun b. Mihran[40] came to the mosque, and then it was said to him, "The men have left!" So he said, "We are Allah's, and to Him are we returning ones! (Qur'an, ii. 151). Truly, the favour of this Worship is more dear to me than the governorship of al-'Iraq!"

Muhammad said, "Whoever does the performances of the Worship forty days in the congregation, with no *takbirat al- ihram*[41] (saying of "Allah is greater" at the beginning of the Worship), escaping him, has Allah ascribed to him two immunities, one from hypocrisy and one from the Fire."

It is said, "On Resurrection Day there will be assembled a people whose faces are like the bright star, so the angels will say to them, 'What were your works?' and then they will answer, 'We were (people who) whenever we heard the Call to Worship, rose for the purification, nothing else preoccupying us'. Then there will be assembled also a group whose faces will be like moons, and they will say, after inquiry, 'We used to perform the ablution before the time (of the Worship).' Then there will be assembled a group whose faces are like the sun, and they will say, 'We used to hear the Call to Worship in the mosque.'"

It is related that the Fathers[42] used to condole themselves

---

39. 'Abdallah b. al-'Abbas, cousin of the Prophet (d. 68, 69 or 70 A.H.).
40. Abu Ayyub Maimun b. Mihran al-Jazari (d. 116 or 117 A.H.).
41. The takbir *al-ihrdm* is so called because its utterance marks the prohibition to the worshipper of what was before permitted to him.
42. *Salaf,* Fathers, in the Divine law is applied to everyone whose tenets, *illadhkab,* are transmitted and whose way, *athar,* is followed, such

three days whenever the first *takbir* ("Allah is greater") escaped them, and they condoled seven days whenever the Congregational Worship escaped them.

The Excellence of the Prostration

The Messenger of Allah said," A creature does not draw near to Allah by anything more excellent than by hidden prostration."

The Messenger of Allah said, "There is no Muslim who prostrates before Allah but Allah raises him a degree by it, and by it puts away from him an evil deed."

It is related that a man said to the Messenger of Allah, "Supplicate Allah that He may make me one of the people of your intercession, and that He may apportion to me fellowship with you in the Garden." He replied, "Help me with numerous prostrations."

It is said, "The nearest a creature is to Allah is when he is prostrating, and that is the meaning of the saying of Allah: 'And prostrate thyself and come near!'" (Qur'an, xcvi. 19).

Allah said, "Their mark is on their faces from the imprint of their prostration" (Qur'an, xlviii. 29). It is said," It is the light of humbleness, for it shines from within on the surface," and that is the soundest meaning. It is also said "It is the brightness that will be in their faces on Resurrection Day from the trace of the ablution."

It is said, "It is that which clings to their faces from the earth when they prostrate."

Muhammad said, "Whenever a son of Adam recites a verse of prostration[43] and then prostrates, Satan moves away, weeping

---

as Abu Hanifah and his companions and their *salaf,* who were the *Sahabah,* Companions of the Prophet, and the Successors, *Tabi'un.* Muhammad is the *muqaddam,* Head of the *Salaf.*

43. Al-Ghazzali gives a brief treatment of the Prostration of the Recital in the seventh section of the second chapter of *Kitab Adab Tilawat al-Qur'an,* "The Book of the Proprieties of the Recital of the Qur'an," Book viii. of the first quarter of the *Ihya'.* He says the "verses of prostration" are fourteen in number, with two in Surat al-Hajj (xxii.), and none in Surah Sad (xxxviii). Sayyid Murtada gives them as follows: vii. 205; xiii. 16; xvi. 52; xvii. 108; xix. 59; xxii. 18, 76;

and saying, "Woe is me! This man was commanded to prostrate and he did so, so he has the Garden; while I was commanded to prostrate[44] (to Adam) but I disobeyed, and so I have the Fire.'"

It is related from 'Ali b. 'Abdallah b. 'Abbas[45] that he used to perform a thousand prostrations every day, and they used to call him "the Prostrator."

It is related that 'Umar b. 'Abd al-'Aziz[46] was wont not to prostrate except on bare earth.

Yusuf b. Asbat[47] used to say, "O company of young men, make use of your health before illness comes, for there does not remain anyone whom I envy except a man who performs completely his bowing and his prostration, since some hindrance has come between me and that."

Sa'id b. Jubair[48] said, "I do not mourn over anything of this life except the prostration."

'Uqbah b. Muslim[49] said, "There is no quality of a creature more beloved with Allah than (that of) a man who loves meeting with Allah, and there is no hour when a man is nearer to Allah than when he kneels in prostration."

---

xxv. 61; xxvii. 25; xxxii, 15; xli. 38 (or 37 or 3); liii. 62; lxxxiv. 21; xcvi. 18. Murtada substitutes xxxviii. 23 for xxii. 76, and objects to liii. 62 and xcvi. 18, because they are commands, as he accepts the rule that the prostration is to be made only when the verses are statements.

44. The story of Iblis's refusal to prostrate before Adam occurs first in the Qur'an at ii. 32, where Baidawi explains the strict theological aspect of it as a prostration to Allah with Adam as *qiblah*.
45. Abu Muhammad and 'Abdallah 'Ali b. 'Abdallah b. 'Abbas b. 'Abd al-Muttalib b. Hashim al-Qarashi al-Hatimi, the ancestor of the Abbasids (d. 117 or 118 A.H.)
46. 'Umar b. 'Abd al-'Aziz al-Umawi, eighth Umayyad khalifah (d. 101 A.H.).
47. Abu Muhammad Yusuf b. Asbat (d. after 190 A.H.).
48. Abu 'Abdallah Sa'id b. Jubair b. Hisham al-Asadi, a Successor (d. 95 or 94 A.H.).
49. 'Uqbah b. Muslim al-Tujibi, *imam* of the congregational mosque of Cairo (d. 243 A.H.). Sometime governor of Egypt.

Abu Hurairah said, "The nearest a creature is to Allah is when he prostrates: so, do much supplication then."

The Excellence of Humbleness

Allah said, "And perform the Worship for remembrance of Me" (Qur'an, xvii. 80; xx. 14; cf. xi 116).

Allah said, "And do not be (one) of the unmindful!" (Qur'an, vii. 204).

He also said, "Do not offer the Worship while you are intoxicated, so that you may know what you are saying!" (Qur'an, iv. 46). It is said' "Intoxicated from the great amount of care," and it is said, "from love of this life." Wahb[50] said, "The thing meant by it is its literal meaning." Anyway, there is a warning in it against being intoxicated with this life, since He shows the defect in it for He said, "so that you may know what you say," and how many a worshipper there is who has not drunk wine, and yet does not know what he says in his Worship!

The Prophet said, "Whoever performs (a Worship of) two *rak'ahs,* without having polluted himself in them with anything of this life, has his previous sinning forgiven him."

The Prophet said, "The Worship is verily humbling and abasing yourself, intercession, crying out and repenting, while you put down your hands and say, 'O Allah, O Allah,' for the worship of one who does not do so is a thing defective."

It is related about Allah (Oh, His praise!), in the former books that He said, "Not from every worshipper do I accept the Worship. I accept the Worship only of him who humbles himself before My greatness and does not exalt himself over Me, and feeds the hungry, needy for the sake of My face."

Muhammad said, "The Worship was prescribed and the Pilgrimage and the Circumambulation (of the Ka'bah) commanded and the pilgrimage ceremonies were enacted as law only to institute remembrance of Allah, so, whenever you do not have any exaltation or awe in your heart for the One Remembered,

---

50. Wahb b. Munabbih, Successor (d. 110 A.H., Sayyid Murtada says here 116.)

Who is the One to be sought and desired, of what value is your remembrance?"

He said to the one to whom he gave an admonition, "And whenever you perform the Worship, make it the Worship of one bidding farewell, i.e. of one bidding farewell to his passions, bidding farewell to his life, and journeying to his Lord, as Allah said, 'O man, you are toiling on toward your Lord indeed, for you are one who shall encounter Him!" (Qur'an lxxxiv. 6).

Allah said: "And fear Allah, and Allah will give you knowledge" (Qur'an, ii. 282). He also said, "And fear Allah, and know that you shall encounter Him!" (Qur'an, ii. 223).

Muhammad said, "Whosoever Worship does not prohibit him from the excessive and the disapproved, has no increase from Allah except of distance."

"The Worship is confidential communion," so how does it exist along with unmindfulness?

Bakr b. 'Abdallah[51] said, "O son of Adam! whenever you will to enter the presence of your Lord without leave and address Him without an interpreter, you enter." He was asked, "And how it is that?" He replied, "You complete your ablution and enter your worship-niche, and behold! you have come before your Lord without leave, and then you address Him without an interpreter."

From 'A'ishah[52] (is this tradition); she said, "The Messenger of Allah used to talk to us and we to him, and when Worship-time came, it was as if he did not know us and we did not know him, so engrossed were we in the greatness of Allah."

Muhammad said, "Allah does not look at the Worship in which a man does not present his heart along with his body."

Whenever Ibrahim the Friend rose for the Worship, the palpitation of his heart used to be heard two miles away.

It happened whenever Sa'id al-Tanukhi[53] worshipped, tears

51. Bakr b. 'Abdallah b. 'Amir b. Hilal al-Muzani al-Basri (d. 108 A.H.).
52. 'A'ishah bint Abu Bakr, the favourite wife of Muhammad (d. 58 A.H.).
53. Sa'id b. Abu Muhammad Sa'id b. 'Abd al-'Aziz b. Yahya al-Tanukhi al-Dimashqi, jurisconsult (d. 168 or 167 A.H.)

did not cease to drop from his cheeks to his beard.

The Messenger of Allah saw a man who was playing with his beard in the Worship, so he said, "If this one's heart were humble, his members would be."

It is related that al-Hasan looked at a man who was playing with pebbles and saying, "O Allah, marry me to the *hur*!"[54] so he said, "A fine suitor you are! Asking in marriage the *hur* while you are playing with stones.!"

Khalaf b. Ayyub[55] was asked, "Do not flies annoy you in your Worship, so that you chase them away?" He replied, "I do not accustom myself to anything that corrupts my Worship." He was asked, "How do you have patience for that?" He replied, "I have heard that criminals exercise patience under the lashings of the sultan, so that it may be said, "Such a one is patient!' and they boast about that. Now, I stand before my Lord: shall I, then, move for a fly?"

It is related about Muslim b. Yasar[56] that he, whenever he wanted to perform the Worship, said to his family, "Go on talking, for I do not hear you."

It is related about him that he was worshipping in the mosque at al-Basrah one day and a side of the mosque fell. Thereupon the people gathered together, but he was not cognizant of it until he withdrew from the Worship.

'Ali b. Abu Talib[57] (may Allah honour his face!), whenever Worship-time came, used to shake, and his face used to change colour. So he was asked, "What is the matter with you, O Commander of the believers?" And he would say, "There has come the time of 'trust' which Allah 'offered to the heavens and the

---

54. The *Ihya'* contains the usual descriptions of the *hur*, the maidens of Paradise, and the Garden (Chapters *Sifat al-Hur, Sifat al-Jannah*).
55. Al-Khalaf b Ayyub al-'Amiri al-Balkhi, *mufti* (d. 209 A.H., according to Sayyid Murtada ; others say 205, 215 or 220 A.H.).
56. Abu 'Abdallah Muslim b. Yasar al-Basri, a Successor, and canon-lawyer (d. 100 A.H.).
57. Abu al-Hasan 'Ali b. Abu Talib 'Abd Manaf b. 'Abd al-Muttalib b. Hashim, cousin and son-in-law of Muhammad and fourth khalifah (d. 40 A.H.).

earth and the mountains, but they refused to bear it and shrank from it' (Qur'an, xxxiii. 72) and I have borne it."

It is related about 'Ali b. al-Husain[58] that it was the case that, whenever he performed the ablution, he became yellow in colour. So his family would say to him, "What is this which befalls you during the ablution?" and so he would reply, "Do you know before whom I wish to stand?"

It is related from Ibn 'Abbas that he said, "Dawud said (in his devotional communion), 'O my God! who will dwell in Thy house, and from whom wilt Thou accept Worship?' And Allah revealed to him, 'O Dawud! only he shall dwell in My house and have his Worship accepted who is humble before My greatness, cuts up his day with remembrance of Me and withdraws himself from fleshly appetities for My sake, giving food to the hungry, sheltering the stranger and showing mercy to the unfortunate. For he it is whose light shall shine in the heavens as the sun. If he call upon Me, I will respond; if he ask of Me, I will give; I will give him, in ignorance, intelligence; in heedlessness, remembrance; and, in darkness, light; and truly he shall be among men like Paradise in the Gardens,[59] whose rivers do not run dry and whose fruit does not change.'"

It is related about Hatim the Deaf that he was asked about his Worship, so he said, "Whenever Worship-time comes I complete the ablution and I go to the place I wish to Worship in, and sit there until my members are composed. Then I rise for the Worship, and place the Ka'bah between my eyebrows and the Bridgeway[60] under my feet with the Garden on my right and the Fire on my left and the Angel of Death behind me and I think it to be my last Worship. Then I stand, between hope and fear, and repeat a *takbir* with precision and recite a recitation that is distinct and bow a bow with humility and make a prostration with self-abasement, and sit on the left thigh and spread on the

58. 'Ali b. Husain Zain al-'Abidin, one of the twelve Shi'ite *imams* (d. 94 A.H.).

59. The other texts, i.e. that on the margin and the Cairo edition of 1334 read "in the highest of the Gardens".

60. In the Qur'an, *Sirat* in most cases refers to "The Straight Road," meaning Islam.

ground the top of its foot and set the right foot on its great toe; then I follow it up with singleness of devotion, and then--I do not know whether it has been accepted or not!"

Ibn 'Abbas said, "A Worship of two *rak'ahs* that are purposed in thought are better than standing a night with the heart heedless."

The Excellence of the Mosque and the Place of Worship.

Allah said, "Only he repairs to the mosques of Allah who believes in Allah and the Last Day" (Qur'an, ix. 18).

Muhammad said, "Whoever builds Allah a mosque, even though it be as the nest of a partridge, will have Allah build a palace for him in the Garden."

He said, "Whoever becomes familiar with a mosque will have Allah become familiar with him."

He also said, "Whenever any of you enters a mosque, let him perform two *rak'ahs* before he sits down."

Muhammad said, "There is no Worship for the neighbour of a mosque except in the mosque."

He said, "The angels intercede for any one of you as long as he is in the place of worship in which he is worshipping, saying, 'O Allah! have mercy[61] on him! O Allah be merciful to him! O Allah! forgive him as long as he does not do anything polluting or go out from the mosque!'"

He also said, "There shall come, in the last time, men of my people who will come to the mosques and sit in them in circles with their thought being of this life and of the love of this life: do not sit with them, for Allah has no need of them!"

Muhammad said, "Allah said in one of the Books, My houses on the earth are the mosques, and My visitors in them are those who repair to them, so, blessed is the creature who purifies himself in his house and then visits Me in My house, for there is a duty upon a host to honour his guest" (cf. Baidawi on Qur'an, ix. 18).

Muhammad said, "Whenever you see a man accustomed to the mosque, testify to his faith."

---

61. The other texts read "What is his right?"

Sa'id b. Musayyab said, "Whoever sits in a mosque truly has fellowship with his Lord, so, how right it is for him not to say anything but good!"

It is related in the Records[62] or the Traditions, "Talking in the mosque devours good works as cattle devour grass."

Al-Nakha'i said, "They used to think that walking to the mosque on a dark night was something that makes the Garden obligatory (as a reward)."

Anas b. Malik[63] said, "Whoever lights a lamp in a mosque has the angels and the bearers of the Throne ceasing not to ask forgiveness for him as long as its light remains in that mosque."

'Ali said, "Whenever a creature dies, the place of his Worship on the earth and the pace of heaven where his work ascends weep over him"; thereupon he recited, "Then the heaven and the earth wept not for them and they were not granted respite" (Qur'an, xliv. 28).

Ibn 'Abbas said, "The earth weeps for him forty mornings."

'Ata' al-Khurasani[64] said, "There is no creature who makes a single prostration to Allah in any one of the places of the earth but will have it testify for him on Resurrection Day and weep for him the day he dies."

Anas b. Malik said, "There is no place in which Allah is mentioned in Worship or Invocation but it boasts over the places around it, and they rejoice in the mention of Allah to their uttermost limit, consisting of seven lands, and there is no creature who stands up for the Worship but has the earth embellished for him."

It is said, "There is no place in which people alight but that place begins to intercede for them or curse them."

---

62. Sayyid Murtada's distinction between *khabar* and *athar* is given in his Introduction to the *Ithaf,* I, 48. The *akhbar* are traditions from the Prophet, while the *athar* are from the Companions and from the Successors and their Successors and the early Fathers after them.
63. Abu Hamzah Anas b. Malik, prolific traditionist (d. 91-93 A.H.).
64. Abu Ayyub (et al, 'Ata' b. Abu Muslim 'Abdallah al-Azdi al-Khurasani al-Balkhi (d. 133 A.H.; Murtada says 135 A.H.).

2

The Manner of Performing the Outward Acts of the Worship

Beginning with the Takbir and What Precedes It

It is fitting that the one performing the Worship, when he finishes the ablution and the cleansing from the uncleanness of body, place and clothing, and the covering of his nakedness from the navel to the knee, should rise, standing facing the *qiblah* outwardly (and the Divine Presence inwardly[65]), and pair[66] his feet together without joining them, for that is one of the things by which they (the Fathers[67]) used to infer a man's legal knowledge.

Muhammad prohibited *safn,*[68] "the raising of the foot," and *safd*, "fettering," in the Worship. "Fettering" is the uniting of the two feet, and this is the meaning of the saying of Allah, "Bound together in fetters" (Qur'an, xiv. 50). *Safn* is the lifting of one of the feet, and this is the meaning of the saying of Allah, "Raising the foot, fleet" (Qur'an, xxxviii. 30). This is what he is to be mindful of as regards his feet when he stands.

He is to be mindful of straightness in his knees and waist, the place of tying his girdle. As for his head, if he will he may

---

65. This is an addition in Sayyid Murtada's text.
66. In this instance the other texts have been translated. Sayyid Murtada reads *yurawiha,* "to stand alternately upon" the feet. But the Cairo 1334 text, and still another Cairo text (of the Matba'ah 'Amirah, 1326) both read *yuzawija,* "to pair," which reads much better.
67. This is supplied by Sayyid Murtada's explanation.
68. The action referred to in the *hadith al-safin* (the noun of action is *sufun*) has two interpretations: (1) joining the feet together, and (2) turning up one foot behind the other as a horse does when it stands upon three feet (*Lisan al-'Arab,* XVII, 116).

keep it erect, and if he will, he may incline it: to incline it appears more humble and more abasing. So let his gaze be fixed on the mat he worships on. If he has no worshipping-mat let him draw near to the encircling wall, or let him draw a line, for that cuts off the extent of his gaze and prevents the scattering of the thought. Let him restrain his gaze from exceeding the edges of his worshipping-mat or the bounds of the line. Let him continue so standing until the Bowing is to be done, without turning. This is the *adab*, Proper Manner, of the *qiyam,* Standing Posture.

Then, whenever his standing and his direction and his extremities are made symmetrical after this fashion, let him recite,[69] "Say, I take refuge with the Lord of mankind" (Qur'an, cxiv.), fortifying himself by it against Satan. Then let him proceed with the Institution of the Worship. If he should hope for the presence of those who would follow his leadership, let him give the Call to Worship first. Next, let him cause the Intention to be present. This means to state an intention, at noon, for instance and say in his heart, "I perform at its proper time the Prescribed Noon Worship to Allah," in order to distinguish it from the *qada'*,[70] "substitute performance," by his saying, "I perform at its proper time," *ada'*; and from the *nafl,* "supererogatory Worship," by saying, "the prescribed," and from the Afternoon or any other Worship, by saying, "noon". Let the meanings of these utterances be present in his heart, for that is the Intention, while the utterances themselves are reminders and causes of its presence.

He strives that that should continue until the end of the *takbir,* so that it may not go away. Then, when that is present in his heart,

---

69. The last two *surahs* are called *al-mu'awwishatan,* because the word *a'udh,* "I take refuge," occurs at the beginning of them. It is a Qur'anic injunction (xvi 100) to begin its recital with such a formula, of which other examples are ii. 63; xi 49; xix. 18; xxiii. 99. 100.

70. *Al-qada'* is setting up one thing in place of another. It is the payment, for cause, of something similar to what was obligatory (Jurjani, *Ta'rifat,* p. 185). Among Shafi'ites, *ada'* and *qada'*, apply especially to the services of worship which have appointed times, and *qada'* is not applied to any performance which may not have a qada', e.g., the Worship of the Feasts and the Friday Congregation. See also note 15 of Chapter 1.

let him raise his hands opposite his shoulders in such a way that his palms will be opposite his shoulders and his thumbs opposite the lobes of his ears (and the tips of his fingers opposite the tops of his ears), so that he may combine the traditions which have come down concerning it. He turns his palms and thumbs towards the *qiblah,* and opens up his fingers, not folding them and not taking pains to separate them or to keep them together, but he lets them be as they naturally are, since there is handed down in tradition both the spreading and the closing (of the fingers), and this is between the two, and so is preferable.

When the hands have come to rest in their position he begins the *takbir* at the same time letting them descend and causing the Intention to be present. Next he places his hands on what is above the naval and below the chest and places the right hand on the left, out of honour for the right hand in that it is the one to be borne. He extends the index and middle fingers of the right hand on the length of the forearm, and takes hold, by the thumb and the little and ring fingers, of the wrist of the left arm.

It has been related that the *takbir* comes along with the raising of the hands, and with their remaining[71] (at the ears) and with their descent. There is nothing wrong with any of these, but I think that it is more suitable that it should be combined with the descent of the hands, for it is the word of binding, since the placing of one of the hands on the other is a form of binding, its beginning being the lowering, and its ending being the placing of them in position. The *takbir*, "Allahu akbar," begins with the "A" and ends with the "r", so it is suitable that there should be regard for the correspondence between the action and the binding. The raising of the hand is, as it were, preliminary to this beginning. Further, it is not fitting that he should raise his hands pushing them forward, nor move them back behind his shoulders, nor shake them to the right or left when he finishes the *takbir*. He lowers them quickly and easily, and commences to place the right one on the left after the lowering.

In one of the narratives it is related that whenever Muhammad said the *takbir*, he would lower his hands, and whenever he wished

71. Sayyid Murtada adds the explanation "they are raised".

to recite, would place the right on the left. If that is sound,[72] it is preferable to what we have mentioned.

As for the *takbir*, it is fitting that he should vocalise the "h" of "Allah" with a light *dhammah* (the vowel "u"), without emphasis, and not insert between the "h" and the "a" any resemblance to a *waw* (the consonant "w"), that being the tendency of emphasising, nor insert between the "b" and the "r" of the "Akbar" an "a", saying "Akbar". He leaves unvowelled the "r" of the "Akbar", not vowelling it with *dhammah*. This is the Form of the *takbir* and what accompanies it.

The Recital

Thereupon he begins the Introductory Supplication. It is well that he should say, after saying, "Allah is greater", "Allah is much greater! Praise belongs to Allah many times over! Oh, the praise of Allah, early and late! I have turned my face to His word, and I am one of the Muslims!" Then he says, "Praise is Thine, O Allah!" and "By Thy Praise! Blessed of itself is Thy name, and exalted is Thy majesty, and sublime is Thy praise, and there is no god but Thee!" that he may combine the variations that have come down in the traditions. If he is behind an *imam*, he is brief, if the *imam* does not have a long pause, in which he recites (the Fatihah).[73]

Then he says: "I seek refuge in Allah from Satan the Stoned."

Next he recites the Fatihah, beginning it with, "In the name of Allah, the Merciful and Compassionate One," giving full value to its doubled and other letters, and striving to differentiate between the dad and the *za*,[74] and he says "*amin*" at the end of the Fatihah. He prolongs it considerably and does not at all join

---

72. Among traditions, *sahih*, "sound", means that the tradition is traced all the way back to Muhammad, is handed down by an unbroken line of honest people, is accurate in imposing or discharging (a duty), and is not exceptional.
73. This is added by Sayyid Murtada as merely a measure of the length of the recital.
74. These are two letters of the Arabic alphabet whose pronunciations among the Arabs or Arabia proper are very similar, but are nevertheless distinguishable.

the "*amin*" to the words, "and not of those going astray". He makes the Recital audible in the morning, at sunset and in the evening, unless he is a follower.[75] He says the "*amin*" audibly.

Next he recites the *surah*, or as much as three verses of the Qur'an, or more, not joining the last of the *surah* with the *takbir* of the bending, but keeping them apart as long as he takes to say, "Oh, the praise of Allah!" He recites in the morning one of the long *surahs of the mufassal*,[76] and at sunset one of the short ones; also at noon and in the afternoon and evening, such as, "By the sky, possessor of the towers!" (lxxxv.) and those near it; and in the morning on a journey, "Say "O unbelievers!"" (cix.), and, "Say, "He is Allah, One!"" (cxii.); and likewise in the two *rak'ahs* of the Dawn,[77] and of the Circumambulation of the Ka'bah, and of the Greeting--with him, during all that, continuing to stand and placing his two hands as we have described at the first of the Worship.

---

75. That is, he is worshipping behind an *imam*.
76. One of the divisions of the Qur'an is into four parts, as follows: (1) *al-tiwal*, "the long," consisting of seven *surahs*, ii. to ix. (which includes viii, because there is no *basmalah* between them), or, others say, ii. to vii, to which are added either x. or xviii. (2) Next to them are *al-mi'um*, "the hundreds," having nearly 100 verses, or more. (3) Next are *al-mathani*, "the duplications," having less than 100 verses. (4) Then come *al-mufassal* (a term derived from Qur'an, xlii. 2), "the divided," because it has numerous section, or "the manifest" (and therefore, also called al-muhkam), because it has few or no abrogated verses in it. This is said to be "the sẹventh seven" (Sayyid Murtada, III, 51C), "the last seven" (Raghib, Al-Mufradat, p. 388), and "the seven of the finals" (Sayyid Murtada, IV, 480). Here the word "seven" refers to the seven-fold division of the Qur'an into portions to be recited; the word is used as a verb in that sense (*Taj al-'Arus*, V, 375A). The *mufassal* is said by most to begin with *surah* xlix., but nine others are mentioned, from xiv to xciii.

    The *mufassal* itself has three sub-divisions, also variously enumerated: (a) *al-tiwal*, "long," xlix-lxxviii., or xlvii-lxxxv., or xlix-lxxx., etc.; (b) *al-awsat*," "medium," to xc. or xciii, or xcvii., etc.; (c) *al-qisar*, "short," to the end.
77. This is the morning *sunnah* Worship, not the prescribed one, which has long *surahs*.

The Bowing and Its Accompaniments

Next he bows, and in the Bowing he observes certain things. These are that he says a *takbir* for the Bowing; and that he raises his hands with the *takbir* of the Bowing and that he prolongs the *takbir* considerably (up to the end of the bow); and that he places the palms of his hands on his knees in the Bowing, with his fingers spread out towards the *qiblah*, on the length of the forelegs; and that he straightens his knees (not doubling them); and that he stretches out his back evenly; and that his neck and head are in line with his back, as one surface, his head not being lower or higher; and that he turns away his elbows from his sides (but a woman keeps her elbows at her sides); and that he says, "Oh the praise of my Mighty Lord!" three times or more, up to seven (or to ten is good, if he is not an *imam*). Next he rises from the Bowing to the Standing Posture, and raises his hands and says, "Allah hears whoever says His praise." He remains at rest in the erect position and says, "Our Lord, Thine is the praise to the fullness of the heavens and the earth and of whatever Thou willest of anything more!" He does not prolong this Standing Posture except in the Worship of the Praise,[78] and of the Eclipse of the Sun,[79] and of the Morning. He recites the *qunut*,[80] in the morning in the second *rak'ah* with the traditional words, before the Prostration.

The Prostration

Next he goes down for the Prostration, saying the *takbir*, and then places his knees on the ground and places his forehead, nose and palms (on the ground), uncovered. He says the *takbir* while lowering himself, but he does not raise his hands in anything but

78. This is the ninth of the Occasional *nafl*, Supererogatory, Worships described by al-Ghazzali.

79. The Worship of Eclipse of the Sun is the first of the Occasional nafl. Worships described by al-Ghazzali.

80. As used by al-Ghazzali, *qunut* is a special supplication, in traditional phrases, added while standing, after the Bowing, in the Prescribed Worship of the Morning and in the *tarawih* Worship of the latter half of Ramadan. Others, however, say there is not *qunut* Supplication except in the morning (al-Bajuri, *Commentary on Abu Shujd*, I, 128D). Sayyid Murtada's discussion is at III, 61 ff.

the Bowing. It is fitting that his knees should be the first to be placed on the ground, and after them his hands, and after them his face; and that he should place his forehead and his nose on the ground; and that he should turn his elbows away from his sides (but a woman should not do that); and that he should keep his feet apart (but a woman should not do that); and that in his Prostration he should leave an open space on the ground (but a woman should not leave a space); "leaving a space" means raising the stomach from the thighs and separating the knees;-- and that he should place his hands on the ground opposite the shoulders, without separating the fingers but rather joining them and joining the thumb to them (but, if he were not to join his thumb, it would not matter); and without extending his arms on the ground, as a dog does, since that is forbidden; and that he should say, "O the praise of my Most High Lord!" three times (but if he increases the number, it is well, unless he is acting as *imam*).

Next he rises from the Prostration, and rests himself a moment in a straight sitting position. So he raises his head, saying the *takbir*, and sits on his left leg and sets up his right foot, and places his hands on his thighs, with the fingers extended, not taking care to close or to separate them. He says, "O Lord, forgive me! Have mercy on me! Provide for me! Guide me! Restore me! Preserve me in health and pardon me." He does not prolong this Sitting[81] except in the Prostration of (the Worship of) the Praise. He makes the second Prostration similarly, and straightens up after it, sitting briefly for the rest in each *rak'ah* not followed by the Witnessing.

Next he stands up: to do so he places his hand on the ground but he does not put either of his legs forward while getting up. He prolongs the *takbir* so that it takes up all the time between the middle of his rising from the Sitting Position to the middle of his rising to the Standing Posture, in such a manner that the "h" of the word "Allah" will come while he is sitting straight, and the "k" of the "akbar" will occur while he is leaning on his hand for the rising, and the "r" of the "akbar" will occur in the middle of his rising for the Standing Posture, so that the *takbir* may fall in the middle of his transition, and only the two extremities

81. See further on this Sitting, Section "The Distinction between the Prescribed Elements and the Usage Portions," below.

(beginning and end of the transition) be free from it (the takbir). This is the most inclusive (application of the varying traditions).

He performs the second *rak'ah* just like the first, and repeats the words "I seek refuge" as at the beginning.

The Witnessing

Next he gives the First Witnessing in the second *rak'ah.* Then he says the Blessing for the Messenger of Allah and for his family. He places his right hand on the right thigh, folding his right fingers, except the index finger, there being no harm in letting loose the thumb also. He points with only the finger of his right hand as he says, "but Allah," not as he says, "There is no god". He sits during this Witnessing on his left foot, as he does between the two Prostrations. In the Last Witnessing he perfects the Supplication mentioned in Tradition for the Prophet. Its *sunan,* Usages, are like the Usages of the First Witnessing, but he sits, in the Last, on his left hip, because he is not ready for the Standing, but rather is to continue there. He places the left foot out from under him (from behind), and sets up the right one. He places the tip of the great toe in the direction of the *qiblah,* if it should not be difficult for him.

Then he says, "The peace is upon you, and the mercy of Allah," and he turns to the right so that his right cheek may be seen from behind on the right side. He turns to the left similarly and gives the Salutation a second time. He has the Intention to leave off the Worship with the Salutation. He has in mind in his Salutation those angels and Muslims who are of his right in the First Salutation, and he has a similar intent in the Second. He makes the Salutation short, and does not prolong it to any extent, as that is the *sunnah,* Usage. This is the Form of the individual Worship.

He raises his voice in the *takbirs,* but he does not raise his voice louder than for himself to hear.

He (the *imam*) states the Intention to do the leading, in order to receive reward. But if he does not state the Intention, the Worship of the people is valid when they state the Intention of imitating him and they will receive the reward of Worship in a congregation.

He says, inaudibly, the Introductory Supplication and the Seeking Refuge, as in the individual Worship, and says, audibly, the Fatihah and the *surah* in each of the Morning, and the first two of the Evening and Sunset *rak'ahs,* and also in the individual Worship. He says the *amin* audibly at the end of the audible[82] Worship, and so does the follower. The follower also says "*amin*" simultaneously with the *imam's amin,* not after him.

The *imam* remains silent after the Fatihah in order that his breath may return to him. The follower recites the Fatihah in the audible Worship during this silence, so that he may be enabled to listen when the *imam* recites. The follower does not recite the *surah* in the audible (Worship), except when he does not hear the voice of the *imam*.

The *imam* says, "Allah hears whoever declares His praise," as he raises his head from the Bowing, and so does the follower. The *imam* does not make more than three repetitions of the Praises of the Bowing and the Prostration, and adds nothing more in the First Witnessing after his saying, "O Lord, have mercy on Muhammad and on the family of Muhammad."

He confines himself in the last two *rak'ahs* to the Fatihah, and is not lengthy for the people. He does not make his Supplication in the Last Witnessing exceed the extent of the Witnessing itself and the Supplication for the Messenger of Allah.

He has in mind, in the Salutation, salutation upon the people and the angels. The people have in mind, in their Salutation, a reply to him.

The *imam* remains still a while, until the people finish the Salutation, and he turns his face towards the people. It is preferable that he remain still, if there are women behind the men, so that the women may depart before him. Not one of the people stands up until the *imam* stands up and departs whither he will to the right or left. I prefer the right.

The *imam* does not particularise himself in the Supplication in the *qunut* of the Morning Worship, but says, "O Allah, guide us!" He says it audibly, and the people say, "*Amin,*" raising their

82. The audible Worships are those of the morning, sunset and evening.

hands opposite their chests. He wipes his face at the close of the Supplications, according to a tradition related about it. Otherwise, analogy would indicate that the hand should not be raised, as at the end of the Witnessing.

Prohibited Things

The Messenger of Allah has forbidden: (a) the raising of the foot in the Worship; (b) the fettering (these we have already mentioned[83]); (c) sitting on the shanks; (d) enveloping; (e) turning up; (f) placing the hands on the sides; (g) placing the hands akimbo; (h) merging; (i) the Worship of one suffering with retention; (j) of the costive; (k) of the pinched; (l) of the hungry; (m) of the angry; and (n) of the muffler, which means one who cover his face.

(c) Sitting, among lexicographers, means sitting on the shanks, lifting the knees and placing the hands on the ground like a dog. Among traditionist it is sitting on the shanks, kneeling, with no part of his on the ground but the tips of the toes and the knees.

(d) Enveloping. The belief of the traditionists about it is that it means that he wraps himself in his garment and puts his hands inside and so bows and prostrates. This was the practice of the Jews in their Worship, and the Muslims were forbidden to imitate them. The shirt is also meant, for it is not fitting that he should bow and prostrate with his hands in the body of his tunic. But it is said to mean placing the middle of the cloak on the head and letting its two sides fall on his right and left, without placing them on his shoulders. The first is nearer right.

(e) Turning up. This is raising his garment before him or behind him when he wishes to prostrate. Sometimes *kaff*, "turning up," is used of the hair of the head, so let no one perform the Worship with his hair twisted. This prohibition applies to men.

In Tradition we read, "I was commanded to prostrate on seven numbers, and not to twist up the hair or the garment."

Ahmad b. Hanbal[84] disliked to put on the *izar*, "inner cloth,"

---

83. See above, beginning of this Chapter.
84. Ahmad b. Muhammad b. Hanbal, celebrated theologian, for whom one of the four schools of canon law is named (d. 241 A.H.).

over the shirt in the Worship, considering it was a case of turning up.

(f) *Al-ikhtisar* is the placing of the hands on the sides.

(g) *Al-salb*[85] is placing the hands on the sides during the Standing Posture and leaving a space between the upper arms and the sides (i.e., standing akimbo).

(h) Merging is of five kinds, two applying to the *imam*, not to merge his Recital with the Opening *takbir*, not his Bowing with his Recital; two applying to the follower, not to merge his Opening *takbir* with the *imam's takbir*, nor his Salutation with the latter's Salutation; one applying to both of them, not to merge the prescribed Salutation with the Second Salutation, but to separate them.

(i) Retention applies to urination.

(j) The costive means the constipated.

(k) A pinched person is one with a tight boot. All of these things hinder humbleness. The same applies to the hungry and the perplexed.

(l) The prohibition of (the Worship of) the hungry is inferred from the words of Muhammad, "Whenever your supper is ready and the Worship has begun, have supper first, unless time presses or you are quite of heart," i.e. can wait until the Worship is finished.

(m) In Tradition we read, "Let not any one of you enter upon the Worship while he is frowning, and let not any one of you enter upon the Worship while he is angry."

Al-Hasan said, "Every Worship in which the heart is not present is swifter to punishment (than to reward[86])."

In Tradition we read, "Seven things in the Worship are due to Satan: nose-bleed, drowsiness, evil suggestions, yawning,

---

85. *Salb* is forbidden because it resembles the position of a man when he is curcified (Lane, *Lexicon*, p. 1711C, quoting *Taj al-'Arus*, I, 338D).

86. This tradition is repeated in the next Chapter (Sayyid Murtada, I, 115) and there Sayyid Murtada adds this additional phrase from the *Qut al-Qulub* of Abu Talib al-Makki. See note 5 to next Chapter.

scratching, turning round, and playing with anything." Some add "unmindfulness and uncertainty."

One of the Fathers said, "Four things in the Worship are coarse: turning round, wiping the face, clearing away pebbles, and worshipping in the path of one who will pass in front of you."

(n) It is also prohibited to interlace the fingers, or to crack the fingers, or to cover the face, or to place one palm against the other and push them between the thighs during the Bowing. Some of the Companions said, "We used to do that and were forbidden it." It is also disliked to blow on the earth during the Prostration, to clean it, and to level the pebbles with the hand, for these are actions that may be dispensed with. He does not raise one of his feet and put it on his thigh, and does not lean in the Standing Posture against a wall, for, if he leans so that he would fall if that wall were drawn away, the most obvious result would be the invalidating of his Worship, and Allah knows better!

The Distinction Between the Prescribed Elements and the Usage Portions

All that we have mentioned applies equally to the *fard,* Prescribed Elements, the *sunnah,* Usage Portions, the *adab,* Properties, and the *hai'at,* Forms, of all the things that it is fitting for the devotee of the way of the next abode to observe.

The Prescribed Elements are twelve in number: (1) The statement of the Intention; (2) the *takbir*; (3) The Standing Posture; (4) the Fatihah; (5) bending down in the Bowing until the palms reach the knees, with coming to rest in it; (6) Straightening from this position, standing; (7) the Prostration, with coming to rest in it, but the placing of the hands (on the ground[87]) is not obligatory; (8) straightening from this, sitting; (9) the Sitting for the Last Witnessing; (10) the Last Witnessing, (11) the Blessing upon the Prophet; (12) the First Salutation.

The statement of the Intention to withdraw from the Worship is not obligatory. Whatever is additional to this is not obligatory, but rather is *sunnah,* Usage, and *hai'at,* Forms, connected with the actions in them, i.e., the *sunnah* and the *fard.*

---

87. This is added in Sayyid Murtada.

The Usages connected with the actions are four (in number): (1) raising the Hands in the Opening *takbir*, and (2) when bending for the Bowing, and (3) when rising for the Standing Posture, and (4) the Sitting for the First Witnessing.

What we have mentioned about the manner of spreading the fingers and the limit of raising them is part of the Forms following this Usage. The sitting on one foot and the laying down of the foot are Forms connected with the Sitting. The lowering of the head and the refraining from turning are Forms connected with the Standing Posture. The beautifying of the external manner of the Standing Posture and the Sitting for Rest,[88] we do not reckon among the fundamental Usages connected with the actions, as they are like the beautifying of the Form of the rising from the Prostration to the Standing Posture. Since they are not purposed in themselves they were not singled out for mention.

The Usages connected with the Invocations are: (1) the Introductory Supplication; (2) the Seeking Refuge;[89] (3) saying "*amin*,"[90] for it is indeed a Confirmed Usage; (4) the Recital of the *surah*; (5) the *takbirs* of the transitions;[91] (6) the Invocation in the Bowing and (7) in the Prostration; (8) the Straightening from them; (9) the First Witnessing, and (10) the Blessing in it upon the Prophet; (11) the Supplication at the end of the Last Witnessing, and (12) the Second Salutation.

These, although we have gathered them all together under the name of *sunnah*, Usage, yet have degrees of gradation, since four of them are made up for by the Oversight Prostration. Of the actions there is one such: it is the First Sitting for the First Witnessing, for it produces an effect, in the carrying out of the order of the Worship, in the eyes of beholders to the extent that there is known by it whether it is a fourfold Worship or not, as opposed to the raising of the hands, for it (the raising of the hands)

---

88. After the Second Prostration in each *rak'ah*, adds Sayyid Murtada.
89. Before the Recital in each *rak'ah*.
90. After the Fatihah.
91. The word adopted to translate *intiqalat* is "transitions," to indicate the changes of position between the Standing, Bowing, Prostration and Sitting postures.

does not produce an effect in changing the order. So it is termed a *ba'd*. Part, of the Worship, and it is said, "The Parts are made good by the Oversight Prostration."

As for the Invocations, only three of them require the Oversight Prostration: (1) the *qunut;* (2) the First Witnessing, and (3) the Blessing upon the Prophet in it, whereas it is just the contrary with the *takbirs* of the transitions and the Invocations in the Bowing and the Prostration and the Straightening from them, because the Bowing and the Prostration, in their external manner, are different from ordinary habit, so the sense of an act of a service of worship is conveyed by them even though there should be omission of the saying of the Invocations, and the *takbirs* of the transitions. The absence of these Invocations does not change the external manner of a service of Worship.

The Sitting for the First Witnessing is a customary action, and was added only for the sake of the Witnessing, so the omitting of it produces a distinct effect.

As for the Opening Supplication and the *surah*, omitting them does not produce an effect, although the Standing Posture has become occupied by the Fatihah and is distinguished from ordinary habit by it.

Likewise the Supplication in the Last Witnessing and in the *qunut* is farthest from what is made good by the Oversight Prostration. But the prolongation of the Straightening in the Morning Worship was enjoined on (the *qunut's*) account, so it is like the prolongation of the Sitting for Rest, since that Sitting became, by the prolongation, along with the Witnessing, the Sitting for the First Witnessing. So this remains a Standing Posture, prolonged, customary, in which there is no obligatory Invocation. And in this description of this Standing Posture as "prolonged", there is a guarding against any other Worship but the Morning, and in its description as "free from any obligatory invocation," there is a guarding against the fundamental character of the Standing Posture in the Worship.

If you say that the distinction between the *sunnah*, Usage, and the *fard*, Prescribed Element, is intelligible, since validity departs with the departure of the Prescribed and not of the Usages, and punishment is faced on account of them, but not on account of the Usages, but, as for the distinction between one *sunnah,* Usage, and another, seeing that all are commanded as being liked, and there is no punishment for omitting all of them, and merit pertains to all of them, what is the meaning of that latter distinction:-- then know that their participation in reward and punishment and desirability does not do away with their gradation. Let us reveal that to you by a similitude. This is that a man is not an existent, perfect man except by means of an inner reality, *ma'na,* together with external members. The inner reality is the life and the spirit. The external are his material members. Further, some of these members are those through whose non-existence the man becomes non-existent, such as the heart, liver and brain, and every other member with the departure of which life departs. Life does not depart on account of some other members, but the purposes of life depart, such as the eye, the hand, the leg, and the tongue. Some of them do not entail departure of life or of the purposes of life, but on their account beauty departs such as the eyebrows, the beard, the eyelashes and a good complexion. Some of them do not entail the departure of the elements of beauty but its perfection, such as the arching of the eyebrows, the blackness of the hair of the beard and the eyelashes, the symmetry of the shape of the members and the commingling of red and white in the complexion. These are degrees of gradation.

So, similarly, worship is a form that the law has made and our devotion is given reality by acquiring it. Its spirit and inner life are humbleness, intention, presence of the heart and singleness of devotion,[92] as shall appear, seeing we are now considering the external parts. So the Bowing, Prostration, Standing Posture and the rest of the Elements act like the heart, head and liver, since the existence of the Worship departs with their departure.

The *sunan,* Usages, we have mentioned, such as the Raising of the hands, the Opening Supplication and the First Witnessing,

---

92. *Al-ikhlas,* "singleness of devotion," with the *salik,* "wayfarer," is the exclusion of *al-khalaq,* "the world," from his dealing with Allah, i.e. he does not act at all except for Allah. It is that all his movements, works and words are for Allah. Its opposite is *shirk,* "associating" something with Allah.

act like the hands, eyes and legs. The validity of the Worship does not depart with their departure, as life does not depart with the departure of these members, but the person becomes, on account of their departure, deformed in shape, blamed and undesirable. Just so, whoever contents himself with the least of what suffices of the Worship is like one who gives to some king a slave that is alive but with his extremities cut off.

The Forms, being those that come after the Usages, act like the causes of beauty, such as the eyebrows, beard, eyelashes and a good complexion.

As for the duties of the Invocations in those Usages, they are the perfectors of beauty, such as the arching of the eyebrows, the roundness of the beard, and so on.

The Worship, for you, is an offering and a valuable present with which you draw near to the presence of the King of kings, such as a young slave-girl, that one seeking proximity to a sultan[93] presents to him. This present is offered to Allah, and then is returned to you on the greatest Presentation Day. So yours is the choice either to make its form beautiful or to make it ugly. If you do well it is for yourself. If you do wrong you wrong your self.

It is not fitting that your pleasure, O lawyer,[94] in the practice of canon law, should be that "Usage is differentiated from Prescribed Element," and then none of the qualities of the Usages are fixed in your understanding but this, that "Abandoning them is allowable and there is no punishment in that," and then you abandon them. For that resembles the saying of the physician, "Putting out the eye does not nullify the existence of a man, but it excludes him (from being a factor) in the realisation of the hope of one seeking to make himself acceptable to the sultan, whenever he brings the one-eyed man as a gift."

Similarly, it is fitting that you should understand the grades of the Usages, Forms and Proprieties, for every Worship whose Bowings and Prostrations a man does not complete will be the

---

93. The other texts have the plural.
94. This is added by Sayyid Murtaḍā in his commentary.

first adversary against its owner, saying, "May Allah neglect you as you have neglected me!" So, study the traditions[95] which we have set forth on perfecting the elements of the Worship, in order that their important position may be apparent to you.

---

95. For these Traditions, see above, Chapter 1, under Section "The Excellences of Performing Completely the Essential Elements".

3

Inward Stipulations For the Acts of the Heart

Let us mention, in this chapter, the close connection of the Worship with humbleness[96] and the presence of the heart.[97] Next let us mention the inner realities, their bounds, causes and treatment. Next let us mention in detail what it is fitting should be present in the heart in every one of the elements of the Worship, that the Worship may be beneficial as provision for the next abode.

Elucidation of the Stipulation[98] for Humbleness and the Presence of the Heart

Know that there are many proofs for this requirement. Among

---

96. Sayyid Murtada remarks here: "Most of the learned, e.g. al-Rafi'i and al-Nawawi, make *khushu'* a *sunnah*, Usage, part of the Worship, while Abu Talib al-Makki and others *make* it a shart, Stipulation, in the Worship, the author, al-Ghazaali, agreeing with them. Some of the Fathers said it was quietness in the Worship, while al-Baghawi said it is submissiveness. Others say it is guidance to the truth, and others say it is the fear that persists in the heart. Abu al-Baqa' said it is humility and demeaning oneself and humbleness toward Allah in the heart and the members. There is difference of opinion as to whether it is one of the works of the heart, or a work of the members, as quietness, or an expression for both. Al-Razi preferred the third alternative."
97. The "heart" is not the seat of the emotions with al-Ghazzali, but rather the seat of his experiential apprehension of the world. It is a transcendant spiritual refinement or subtlety. Its connection with the physical heart has been the despair of the minds of men. For al-Ghazzali's use of the word, see Sayyid Murtada, I, 331; VII, 201 ff.
98. The *shart*, "Stipulation," of a thing is something upon which the soundness of the thing depends, but which is not a *juz'*, "part," of

them is the saying of Allah, "Institute the Worship for remembrance of Me" (Qur'an, xvli. 80). The evident meaning of a command is its obligation. Now, unmindfulness is the opposite of remembering, and so, how can who is unmindful in all his Worship be an institutor of the Worship for remembrance of Him?

Likewise, the saying of Allah, "And do not be of the unmindful!" (Qur'an, vii. 204), is a prohibition, and the evident meaning of it is to make unlawful.

The saying of Allah, "So that you may know what you are saying" (Qur'an, iv. 46), is an assignment of a motive for the prohibition of inebriety, and it is also of general application to the unmindful, anxiously engrossed in evil suggestions and thoughts of this life.

The saying of Muhammad, "The Worship is verily humbling and abasing oneself," is restrictive on account of the definite article. The word "verily" is for confirmation and emphasis. The canon lawyers have understood the saying of Muhammad, "The right of pre-emption verily applies to what has not been divided," as meaning restriction, affirmation and negation.

The saying of Muhammad, "Whosoever Worship does not prohibit him from the excessive and the disapproved has no increase from Allah except of distance," applies, seeing that the Worship of the unmindful does not prohibit from the excessive and the disapproved.

Muhammad said, "How many standing up will have as their portion from their Worship only fatigue and misfortune!" and he meant by that none other than the unmindful.

He said, "A creature gets from his Worship only what he comprehends of it." The verification of this is in the fact that the worshipper is in communion with his Lord, as the tradition about it has declared, and speech with inattention is not communion at all. The demonstration of that is in the fact that the quarter-tithe, if a man is unmindful of it, for instance, is still, in itself, opposed

---

the thing. By this definition of the *rukn*, "essential element," is excluded from the term *shart*, for it is a *juz'*, "part", of the Worship (al-Bajuri, *Commentary on Ibn Shuja't*, I, 142B).

to his natural craving and oppressive to the lower self. Likewise fasting overcomes the physical powers, breaking the dominion of the fleshly inclination, which is an instrument of Satan's, the enemy of Allah. So it is not strange that which is intended should be secured from them (the quarter-tithe and fasting), in spite of unmindfulness. Likewise the activities of the Pilgrimage are a great hardship, and entail from the exertion something from which suffering results, whether the heart is present with its activities or not.

Now, the Worship comprises only Invocation and Recital, Bowing and Prostration, Standing and Sitting The Invocation is conversation and communion with Allah. Then, either the object of it is its being an address and a conversation, or the object of it is the letters and the sounds for the sake of testing the tongue by the exercise, just as the stomach is tested by restraint in the fast, and as the body is tested by the hardships of giving out the quarter-tithe and parting with property that is exceedingly dear. There is no doubt that this character of the Worship is invalid, for the moving of the tongue in nonsense is easy for the unmindful! For there is no testing in it in so far as it is an exercise. The object is not utterance by means of the letters because it is simply utterance, but because it is beneficial utterance, and it becomes beneficial utterance only whenever it expresses what is in the mind, and it becomes such an expression only by the presence of the heart. Thus, what request is there in the saying, "Guide us into the Straight Road!" (Qur'an, i. 5), when the heart is unmindful and when one does not intend that it should be an intercession and a supplication? For what hardship is there in moving the tongue with it, along with unmindfulness, especially after it has become customary?

This is the rule for the Invocations. Nay more, I say, were a man to take an oath, saying, "I will indeed thank such a one, and praise him, and ask him for some need," and then have the expressions indicating these meanings pass over his tongue in his sleep, he would not have fulfilled his oath. Were they to pass over his tongue in the darkness, with that man present, but without the first knowing of his presence or seeing him, he would not have fulfilled his oath, since his speech would not be an address, and talking with him, as long as he (the second) was not present in his (the first's) heart. Even were these words to pass over his tongue while he is present, with himself, though it is daylight, nevertheless unmindful of him because he is submerged in some anxious thought or other, having no purpose of presenting the address to him as he spoke he would not have fulfilled his oath.

Now there is no doubt that the object of the Recital and the Invocations is praise and lauding, intercession and supplication, and the One addressed is Allah, even though the heart, by the veil of unmindfulness, is hidden from Him. He does not see Allah or observe Him, so is unmindful of the One addressed, but his tongue moves in accordance with habit. How far this is from the object of the Worship, which was enjoined in order to give lustre to the heart, and to renew the remembrance of Allah, and in order that the bond of faith in Him may be established!

This is the rule of the Recital and the Invocation. In brief, there is no way to deny this property (of unmindfulness in the Worship) to the speech part of it, or to differentiate it from the act.

As for the Bowing and Prostration, their object is to magnify, absolutely. If it were possible for one to be a magnifier of Allah by his action, while he is unmindful of Him, then it would be possible for him to be a magnifier of an idol placed in front of him, while he is unmindful of it, or for him to be a magnifier of a wall in front of him, while he is unmindful of it.

Whenever the act ceases to be magnifying, nothing remains but the movement of the back and head. There is no hardship in that, the purpose of which could be testing, and which would make it "the support of the religion," so that it decides between unbelief and Islam, and takes precedence over the Pilgrimage and other religious services, and is something on whose account killing is obligatory when it is abandoned intentionally. I do not think that all this importance belongs to the Worship because of its external acts, unless there is connected with them the object of communion, for that takes precedence over fasting, quarter-tithes, Pilgrimage and anything else, nay, even sacrifices and offerings, which are a warring against the flesh because they decrease wealth. Allah said, "Assuredly their flesh and their blood will not reach Allah, but wary fear on your part reaches Him" (Qur'an, xxii.

38), that is, the quality that rules over the heart to the extent that it induces the heart to obey the commands, is what is desired. For of what sort is a command to perform the Worship if there is no need to perform its component actions? So then, as regards the inner reality of the Worship, this is what points to the requirement of the presence of the heart.

Were you to say, "If you pronounce the Worship to be invalid, seeing that you make the presence of the heart a stipulation for its validity, then you go against the agreement of the canon lawyers, since they have stipulated for the presence of the heart only at the *takbir*," then know that I have already said in the Book of Knowledge (Book I of the *Ihya'*), that canon lawyers do not concern themselves with what is within, and are not troubled about hearts or the way of the next abode. Rather, they build up the external side of the laws of the religion upon the external side of the acts of the members, since the external side of the acts is a sufficient guard against being killed or chastised by the *sultan*.

As to whether the external side of these acts benefits in the next abode, this is not within the bounds of canon law, because it is not possible to claim agreement on this point.

It has been handed down from Bishr b. al-Harith,[99] in what Abu Talib[100] related from him by oral tradition from Sufyan al-Thawri,[101] that he said, "The Worship of anyone who is not humble is invalid."

It is related from al-Hasan that he said, "Every Worship in which the heart is not present is swifter to punishment (than to reward)."

From Ma'adh b. Jabal[102] it is related, "Whoever acquaints himself with the one who is on his right or his left, purposely,

---

99. Abu Nasar Bishr al-Hafi b. al-Harith al-Marwazi (d. 226-27 A.H.).
100. Abu Talib Muhammad b. 'Al b. 'Atiyah al-Harithi al-Wa'iz al-Makki (d. 386 A.H.), author of the *Qut al-Qulub*, Sufi reference book, upon which al-Ghazzali based the Ihya' (sayyid Murtada, I, 134; Nicholson, *A Literary History of the Arabs*, p. 338).
101. Abu 'Abdallah Sufyan b. Sa'id al-Thawri (d. 161 A.H.).
102. Ma'adh b. Jabal, al-Khazraji. Helper, foremost *imam* in the knowledge of allowed and prohibited things (d. 17 A.H.).

while he is at Worship, has no Worship."

There is related also this tradition with a complete *isnad,*[103] or chain of authorities, "Truly, a creature may offer Worship of which not a sixth or a tenth is written down for his credit," and "There is written down for a creature's credit only what he comprehends of his Worship." This, were it related from anyone else, would have been made a tenet, so why is it not held to?

'Abd al-Wahid b. Zaid,[104] said, "The learned agree that there is nothing of the Worship reckoned to a creature except what he comprehends." So he made it a matter of Agreement.[105] What is related along these lines from the scrupulous canon lawyers and from the learned of the next world is more than can be reckoned.

The right thing is to return to the legal proofs, seeing that the Traditions and the Records,[106] are clear as to this Stipulation, with this proviso, that the standing of a *fatwa,* "legal opinion," in regard to an external duty is restricted by the measure of the deficiency of mankind. For it is not possible to place Stipulations upon men for the presence of the heart in the entire Worship, for only the fewest of mankind are capable of doing that. Since the Stipulation of total comprehension is, of necessity, not possible, it is unavoidable for him that he should require as little of it as the name would apply to, were it only of the duration of a glance, the most preferable moment for it (the presence) being the moment of the *takbir.*

So we limited ourselves to laying down that as a duty, hoping, along with that, that the state of the unmindful in all his Worship may not be like the state of one abandoning it altogether, for he, on the whole, is more eager to perform the Worship outwardly,

---

103. Sayyid Murtada adds: "He means that it is traced back to the Prophet".

104. 'Abd al-Wahid b. Zaid al-Basri (Abu 'Ubaidah) (d. 128 a.h.), (Ibn Nadim, *Al-Fihrist,* p. 183).

105. *Al-ijma'* is the agreement of the *mujtahids,*"those who by reason of religious learning have the right to pronounce an opinion, of the people of Muhammad in any age upon any religious matter (Jurjani, *Ta'rifat,* p. 9).

106. Sayyid Murtada reads here "verses" but he mentions the other reading in his comment.

and has his heart present more than the other for a moment. And why should it not be so, seeing that the Worship of one who worships while ceremonially unclean, through forgetfulness, is invalid with Allāh, nevertheless he gets a certain amount of reward, according to his act and the measure of his deficiency and his excuse?

But, in spite of this hope, we[107] fear that his state may be worse than the state of one abandoning it altogether; and why not, since the one who presents service, but treats the Divine Majesty with contempt, and speaks the speech of the unmindful and the disdainful, is in a worse state than the one who turns away from the service? Whenever the causes of fear and hope oppose each other, and the matter becomes dangerous in itself, then you must make your choice afterwards between taking it seriously and taking it lightly.

For all that, it is not desired to oppose the canon lawyers in their rulings concerning the validity of the Worship along with unmindfulness, for that is the necessary character of the *fatwa*, "judicial opinion," as has been noted. Whoever knows the inner reality of the Worship knows that unmindfulness contradicts it. But we have mentioned in the chapter on "The Difference between Superficial and Mystic Knowledge,"[108] in the "Book of the Foundations of the Articles of the Faith," that the deficiency of mankind is one of the causes hindering the clear exposition of all that may be revealed of the mysteries of the law. So let us content ourselves with this measure of discussion, for in it is sufficient for the devotee seeking the way of the next abode, but the factious disputer we do not intend to argue with now.

The result of the discussion is that the presence of the heart is the spirit of the Worship, and that the least of that by which the last gasp of the spirit remains is the presence at the *takbir*, and less than it is ruin. According to the measure of the increase over it, the spirit extends into the other parts of the Worship.

---

107. The other texts have "he".
108. There are three knowledges: *zahir*, "surface, superficial," for the populace; *batin*, "inner, mystic," reserved for those who are worthy, and private, which is between Allah and himself and which he discloses to on one.

How many loving there are, without movement, really dead! For the Worship of the unmindful in all except the *takbir* is like one alive, but without movement. We ask Allah for His excellent help!

Exposition of the Inner Realities by which the Life of the Worship is Distinguished[109]

Know that for these inner realities there are many modes of expression, but six phrases will comprehend them. These are: (a) the presence of the heart; (b) apprehension; (c) magnifying; (d) awe; (e) hope, and (f) shamefacedness. So let us give detailed statements of them; next of their causes, and then of the treatment for acquiring them.

Now for the details. (a) First, the presence of the heart. By this we mean that the heart is free from everything but what the worshipper is engaged in and what he utters, so that the work[110] may be associated with both the acts and the words, and that the thought may not be wandering to other things. Whenever the thought turns away from what it is not engaged in, and there is in one's heart remembrance of what he is about, and he is not unmindful of anything, the presence of the heart results.

(b) But the apprehension of the significance of the word is a matter that comes after the presence of the heart. For it may be that the heart is present with the utterance, but not present with the significance of the utterance. So the heart's comprehension of the significance of the utterance is what we meant by "apprehension". This is a place where men differ, since men do not share in the apprehension of the significations of the Recital and Praisings. How many subtle significations the worshipper understands during the Worship which did not occur to his heart before! From this point of view the Worship becomes a "restrainer from the excessive and the disapproved,"[111] for it gives understanding of matters, and these matters forbid the excessive and the disapproved inevitably.

(c) The magnifying is a matter which comes after the presence of the heart and the understanding, since a man addresses to his

---

109. The other texts have "perfected".
110. The other texts have "the knowledge".
111. This is an allusion to Qur'an, xxix. 44.

slave words in which his heart is present and of which he apprehends the meaning, but he does not magnify him. So magnifying is additional to them.

(d) The awe is something additional to magnifying; rather, it is an expression for fear whose source is magnifying, for whoever does not fear is not called full of awe, seeing that fear of the scorpion, and of the evil nature of mankind, and of similar low causes of fear, is not called awe, but fear of a magnified sultan is called awe, for awe is fear whose source is majesty.

(e) As for hope, there is no doubt that it is additional. How many there are who magnify some king, are in awe of him, and fear his might, but they do not hope to be rewarded by him! So it is fitting that the creature should be hopeful, on account of his Worship, of the reward of Allah, as he is fearful, on account of his deficiency, of the punishment of Allah.

(f) Shamefacedness is additional to the whole, for its basis is the feeling of deficiency and the supposition of guilt. Exaltation, magnifying, fear and hope may be conceived of, without shame, where there is no supposition of deficiency and committing of sin.

Now for the causes of these six inner realities. Know that the cause of the presence of the heart is your solicitude about it, for your heart follows your solicitude. For your heart is present only in what you are solicitous about. Whenever a matter is one of solicitude to you, your heart is there present, willingly or unwillingly, for it is constituted that way, and is under compulsion in it. The heart, whenever it is not present in the Worship, is not without employment, but rather is roaming about in whatever matters of this life one's solicitude is turned to. So there is no expedient and no treatment for the presence of the heart except through turning one's solicitude to the Worship, for solicitude is not directed to the Worship, as long as it is not clear that the object desired depends on the Worship. That includes faith and assurance that the next abode is better and more lasting, and that the Worship is a means of reaching it. So, whenever this faith is joined to real knowledge of the insignificance of this life and its chief concerns, there results from their association the presence of the heart in the Worship. By means similar to this your heart is present whenever you come before some great people who are not able to harm or benefit you. So, whenever it happens that it is not present during communion with the King of kings, in Whose hands are the Seen and the Unseen Worlds,[112] and benefit and bane, do not suppose that there is any other reason than weakness of faith. So be zealous now to strengthen faith. The way to it will be gone into elsewhere.

As for the apprehension, the cause of it, after the presence of the heart, is persevering in thinking and turning the mind to the comprehension of the significance (of the purpose[113]). The treatment for it is whatever is a treatment for the presence of the heart, together with turning towards thinking and exerting oneself in repelling idle fancies. The treatment for repelling engrossing fancies is to cut off the materials out of which they spring. I mean, abstaining from those causes to which one's thoughts are attracted. As long as those materials are not cut off, idle fancies will not turn away from them. For, whoever loves a thing increases his remembrance of it, and remembrance of what is beloved rushes upon the heart inevitably, and therefore you see that whoever loves another than Allah does not have a single act of Worship free from idle fancies.

The magnifying is a state of the heart born of two cognitions, one of which is the knowledge of the majesty and greatness of Allah. This is one of the fundamentals of the faith, for whoever does not believe in His greatness has a self which does not submit to magnifying Him. The second is the knowledge of the insignificance of the self, and of its vileness, of its being a creature, under compulsion, lorded over, to the point that there is born of these two knowledges submission, brokenness and humbleness towards Allah, and that is what is meant by magnifying. As long as knowledge of the insignificance of the self is not commingled with knowledge of the majesty of Allah, the state of magnifying

112. The *'alam al-malakut* is the World of the Unseen, applying especially to the spirits of the selves (Sayyid Murtada, I, 63D). In *Al-Insan al-Kamil* every existing thing is divided among three classes, the outward class, which is termed *al-mulk,* the inner class, which is called al-malakut and the third class, which is exclusive of the first two, and it is *al-jabarut al-Ilahi.* See also Sayyid Murtada, I, 173.
113. This is added by Sayyid Murtada.

and humbleness is not attained. For, the one who needs no other, and trusts to himself, may recognise qualities of majesty in someone else, without his state being one of humbleness and magnifying, because the other counterpart, which is the knowledge of the insignificance of the self and its need, was not joined to it.

As for awe and fear, that is a state of the self born of one's knowledge of the power and might of Allah, and of the execution of His will in him, with small regard for him, and of the knowledge that, were He to destroy the first and the last,[114] He would not diminish His dominion a particle. This holds along with observation of the misfortunes and various trails that happen to prophets and saints, in spite of the power (of Allah) to repel them, as opposed to what is seen among earthly kings. In brief, whenever the knowledge of Allah increases, fear and awe increase. The causes of that will follow in the Book of Fear, of the Quarter of the *Ihya* on Saving Matters.

As for hope, its cause is knowledge of the graciousness of Allah, His generosity, the universality. His bestowing of kindnesses, of the favours of His work, and also the knowledge of His truthfulness in His promise of the Garden in exchange for Worship. So, whenever certain assurance of His promise and knowledge of His graciousness result, hope issues from their association, inevitably.

As for shamefacedness, its cause is in one's sense of deficiency in religious service, and one's knowledge of one's inability to perform the great right of Allah. It grows strong through knowledge of the blemishes and faults of the self, the littleness of its sincere devotion, the vileness of its inner nature, and its inclination to what is fleeting in all its actions, in spite of the knowledge of the great things that the majesty of Allah requires, along with the knowledge that He is an observer of the secret thoughts and the idle fancies of the heart, although they are subtle and hidden. Whenever these cognitions assuredly result, there is sent forth from them a state called shamefacedness.

So these are causes of these qualities. If the securing of anything is desired, the treatment is to make its cause to be present, for the knowledge of its cause is the knowledge of the treatment

114. The reference is to Qur'an lxxvii. 16-17.

for securing it. The bond of connection in all these causes is faith and assurance; by faith, I mean those cognitions which we have mentioned, and the meaning of their being assured is the denial of doubt, and their taking complete rule over the heart, as has preceded in the exposition of Assurance in the Book of Knowledge. According to the measure of assurance the heart is humble.

For that reason 'A'ishah said, "The Messenger of Allah used to talk to us and we to him, and when Worship time came, it was as if he did not recognise us and we did not recognise him."

It is related that Allah revealed to Moses, "O Moses, whenever you make mention of Me, mention Me while you are shaking in your members, and while mentioning Me, be humble and composed, and whenever you mention Me, keep your tongue behind your heart, and whenever you stand before Me, stand as humble slave, and commune with Me with a timorous heart and a truthful tongue."

It is related that Allah revealed to him, "Say to the rebellious of thy people, 'They shall not mention Me, for I have taken an oath upon Myself, that I will mention whoever mentions Me, so whenever they mention Me, I will mention them with a curse.'" This applies to one disobedient but not unmindful in his mentioning, and who will it be when unmindfulness and disobedience are joined together?

In accordance with the diversities of the inner realities in the hearts which we have mentioned, men are divided into the unmindful who completes his Worship, but whose heart is not present in a single moment of it, and the one who completes it with his heart not absent a single moment, nay, rather, he may perhaps be so completely solicitous about it that he does not perceive what happens in front of him. On that account Muslim b. Yasar did not perceive the falling of a column in the mosque about which men gathered. One of them used to attend the Congregational Worship for a long time and never recognised at all who was on his right and on his left. The palpitation of the heart of Ibrahim (the mercies and peace of Allah be upon him) used to be heard two miles. A company used to turn yellow of face and to tremble in their shoulder muscles. All that is not improbable, for double of it is seen in the concern of the people of the world and in fear of the kings of the earth, for all their impotence their weakness and the vileness of the bits of fortune that may be secured from them, so that one may come before a king or a minister and address him concerning his matter of importance and then go out, and, were he asked about those around him, or about the king's raiment, he customarily would not be able to give information about it, because of the preoccupation of his concern with the king himself, rather than his raiment, or those present around him.

So for all degrees of what men do, the portion of everyone from his Worship is according to the measure of his fear, his humbleness and his magnifying. For, the place where the gaze of Allah falls is the hearts, not the outward movements. For that reason one of the Companions said, "On Resurrection Day mankind will be assembled in accordance with the pattern of their forms in the Worship, consisting of composure, quietness and the existence of delight and pleasure in it." He surely spoke the truth, for everyone will be assembled according as he died, and die according as he lived, and in that the state of his heart will be considered, not the state of his person. So, form the qualities of the heart will the forms be fashioned in the next abode. No one will escape except him who brings to Allah a sound heart.

We ask! Allah for His excellent success, by His kindness and generosity.

Exposition of the Remedy Beneficial for the Presence of the Heart

Know that the believer must be a magnifier of Allah, be in fear of Him, hopeful towards Him and ashamed of his shortcoming: one must consequently not become free of these states after becoming a believer in Islam. And if the strength (of the states[115]) is in proportion to the strength of his assurance, his departure from them in the Worship can have no cause except (a) scattering of thought, (b) division of interest, (c) the absence of the heart from the communion, or (d) unmindfulness towards the Worship. Nothing disturbs from the Worship except invading, engrossing fancies.

---

115. This is by added Sayyid Murtada.

The remedies for the presence of the heart is the repelling of those fancies. The thing itself is not repelled except by the repelling of its cause, so, learn its cause. The cause for the coming together of engrossing fancies is either some external matter, or a matter that is itself inward.

The external thing may be what strikes the hearing or appears to the sight, for that sometimes snatches away the attention, so that if follows the thing and busies itself with it. Then the thought is drawn away to something else and it goes linking on. Likewise the sight of things becomes a cause of thought about them, and then some of those thoughts give rise to others. But for him whose intention is strong and whose solicitude is lofty, what occurs to his senses does not occupy him. Bur for one who is weak it is a matter of course that his thought branches off on it. The remedy for that is cutting off these causes, by lowering the gaze, or worshipping in a dark house, or by not leaving before one what will engage his sense, or by drawing near to a wall in his Worship, so that the range of his vision may not be extended, and guarding against Worship in the streets and in places decorated and worked, and on dyed carpet. For that reason the devotees[116] used to worship in a small, dark house, just large enough for prostration, that their attention might be more concentrated. The strongest ones among them used to be present in the mosques and to lower their gaze and not to let it pass the place of prostration, and to consider that the perfection of Worship consisted in not recognising those who were on their right or left. Ibn 'Umar[117] would not leave in the place of Worship either a book or a sword without removing them, nor any writing without erasing it.

The inward causes are more difficult, for he whose concerns carry him off into the vales of the earth is one whose thinking is not confined in one department--rather he does not cease to fly from one side to another. The lowering of the gaze is of no use to him, for what took place in the heart previously is sufficient for the preoccupation. So this is the way for him: let him restore the self forcibly to an understanding of what he is reciting in the

116. These are the *sufi* masters, says Sayyid Murtada.

117. 'Abdallah b. 'Umar b. al-Khattab, Companion, son of the second Khalifah (d. 73 A.H.; Sayyid Murtada says 75 A.H.).

Worship, and employ himself in this rather than anything else. It will help him to do that if he prepares for it before the Opening *takbir* by renewing to himself the remembrance of the next abode, the place of communion where he is, and the peril of his position before Allah, which is a place of perception (of things of the next abode[118]). He empties his heart, before entering upon the Worship, of whatever he is solicitous about, and does not leave to his lower self any business to which his interest may turn.

The Messenger of Allah said to 'Uthman b. Abu Shaibah,[119] "I forgot to tell you to cover the two horns[120] which are in the House of Allah, for it is not fitting that there should be in the House of anything that disturbs men from their Worship."

This is the way to quite the thoughts. Then, if the thing that excites one's thoughts does not quiet down by this quieting remedy, nothing will save him except the purge that drains the matter of the disease from the deepest veins. This is to look into the matters turning him away and preoccupying him from the presenting of the heart. There is no doubt that they have reference to his chief concerns, and they have become the things of importance only on account of his desires. So he chastises his lower self by breaking away from those desires and cutting off those bonds. For, whatever preoccupies him from his Worship is an opponent of his religion, and is of the army of Satan, his enemy. Holding on to it is more harmful for him than casting it out, for he saves himself from it by casting it out, just as it is related that Muhammad put on the black robe which Abu Jahm[121] brought him, and which had a border on it, and worshipped in it and then took it off after his Worship and said, "Take it to Abu Jahm, for it distracted me a while ago from my Worship, and bring me Abu Jahm's coarse

---

118. This is added by Sayyid Murtada.
119. Sayyid Murtada omits the Abu before Shaibah. Al-'Iraqi (d. 806 A.H.), the author who worked on the sources of al-Ghazzali's traditions, says this tradition is not from 'Uthman b. Shaibah, but from 'Uthman b. Talhah al-Hajabi, the keeper of the Ka'bah, who is reported in Ibn Hajar's *Biographical Dictionary,* II, 1097 f. (d. 42 A.H.).
120. The other texts read "cooking pot".
121. Abu Jahm 'Amir b. Hudhaifah al-'Adari al-Qarashi al Madani (d. 60 A.H.).

woollen garment."

The Messenger of Allah ordered a renewal of the strap of his sandal, and then looked at it during his Worship, since it was new, and then ordered it to be taken off of it and the worn-out strap to be restored.

He had put on some sandals and their excellence pleased him. So he performed a Prostration. Then he said, "I humbled myself before my Lord, that He might not detest me." Then he went out with them and delivered them to the first beggar he met. Then he ordered 'Ali to buy him two smooth raw-hide sandals, and he wore them.

He had a gold ring on his hand before it was made unlawful while he was in the pulpit, and he threw it away, saying, "This occupied me with one look at it and one look at you."

It is related that Abu Talhah[122] worshipped in an enclosure he had, in which were trees. Then a wood-pigeon flew among the trees, looking for an exit, and his sight followed it awhile. Then he did not know how many *rak'ahs* he had performed. So he mentioned to the Messenger of Allah what had occurred to him and then said, "It is an alms, so put it wherever you wish."

It is related of another man that he worshipped in an enclosure belonging to him, while the date-palms were encircled by their fruit, and he looked at them and they pleased him. So he mentioned that to 'Uthman and said, "It is alms, so make use of it in the path of Allah." So 'Uthman sold it for fifty thousand. They were accustomed to do that, cutting off the matter they thought about, and it was an atonement for whatever deficiency of the worship had occurred.

This is the remedy that overcomes the disease, when nothing else suffices. For, what we have mentioned concerning what is favourable for giving quietness and causing a return to an understanding of the remembrance, is beneficial with weak desires and cares which do not occupy more than the margin of the heart. But quieting does not benefit the strong, overcoming desires.

---

122. Abu Talhah Zaid b. Sahl b. Aswad b. Kharam al-Madani, Helper (d. 51 A.H.).

Rather, they continue to attract you, and all your worship comes to an end in the occupation of pulling this way and that. It is like a man under a tree who wants to do some clear thinking for himself. Then the voices of the sparrows disturb him, and he continually drives them away with a stick in his hand and returns to his thinking. Then the sparrows return and he repeats striking at them with his stick. Then it is said to him, "This is the proceeding of a water wheel, and does not end. If you wish salvation, cut down the tree." So likewise the tree of the desires, whenever it spreads out and its branches extend themselves, has thoughts attracted to it as sparrows are attracted to trees and as flies are attracted to filth, and the business of getting rid of them is a long one. For, a fly, as often as it is repelled, returns, and for that reason it is called *dhubab*,[123] something that is repelled and returns.

So likewise the stray thoughts and desires are numerous, and rarely is a creature free from them. There is one root that includes them all, and that is love of this life. "That is the head of all sin," the foundation of all deficiency and the source of all wickedness. Let not the man, whose heart harbours love of this life so that he inclines to it for its own sake, and not in order to provide for his journey, nor to seek aid, by means of it, for the next abode, hope that the pleasure of communion in the Worship will be clear to him. For, whoever rejoices in this life will not rejoice in Allah and in communion with Him. The solicitude of a man is for that by which his eye is refreshed. If that by which his eye is refreshed in this life, inevitably his concern goes out to it. Yet, for all that, it is not fitting that he should leave off the struggle to turn the heart to the Worship to reduce the disturbing causes, for this is the bitter remedy. On account of its bitterness the natural disposition abhors it. The illness remains chronic, and the disease becomes difficult to cure, so that the elders were zealous to Worship two *rak'ahs* without letting anything worldly occur to themselves in them, but were unable to do that. So it is not for people like us to have desire for that,

---

123. Dhabb means "he repelled" and *ab* means "he returned," but Sayyid Murtada refuses to accept this bit of etymology, and refers to his dictionary, the *Taj al-'Arus*.

but, would that half or a third of the Worship were preserved for us from distractions, that we may be of those who mingle a good work with another thing that is bad! In brief, the solicitude of this life and solicitude for the next abode are in the heart like water which is poured into a vessel full of sesame oil.[124] According to the amount of water that enters into it the oil goes out, inevitably, for they do not mix.

Detailed Exposition of What it is Fitting Should be Present in the Heart at Every Element and Stipulation of the Acts of the Worship

We say, it is your duty, if you are among the seekers of the next abode, not to be unmindful, first, of the admonitions which are in the Stipulations and the Elements of the Worship.

The Preliminary Stipulations[125] are: the Call to Worship, the Purification, the Covering of the person, Facing the *qiblah*, Standing erect and the Intention. So, whenever you hear the Call of the *mu'adhdhin*, present to your heart the dread of the Call on Resurrection Day, and prepare yourself outwardly and inwardly for replying and hastening, for, those who hasten to this Call are those who are called in favour on the greatest Presentation Day. So, apply your heart to this Call, and, if you find it full of joy and rejoicing, laden with desire to hasten, know that the Call brings you glad tidings and deliverance on the Day of Judgment. For that reason Muhammad said, "Rest us, O Bilal!"[126] that it, "Rest us by it, and by the Call to it," since the refreshing[127] of his eye was in it.

As for the Purification, whenever you purify your place, which is your outermost container, and then your clothing, which is your nearest covering, and then your skin, which is your closest shell, do not be unmindful of your kernel, which is your essence, and that is your heart. So, exert yourself on its behalf, cleansing it

---

124. The other texts read *khall*, "vinegar," instead of *hall*.
125. These Preliminary Stipulations, says Sayyid Murtada, are *sunnah*, thus excluding them from the *fard'id* class of the parts of the Worship.
126. Bilal b. Rabah al-Habashi (Abyssinian), the first mu'adhdhin (d. 20 A.H.).
127. This is a Qur'anic expression, xxviii, 8; also xxv. 74, xxxii. 17.

by repentance and remorse for previous acts, renewing the resolve to abandon such things, in the future. So cleanse by repentance your inward parts, for that is the place the One you worship observes.

As for the Covering of the person, know that it meant to cover the shameful things of the body from the gaze of people, for the outward part of your body is the place people observe. And what is your opinion about the disgraceful things of your inner self, and the dishonourable things of your secret thoughts, which no one gazes upon but your Lord? So present these disgraceful things to your mind, and ask yourself to cover them, but be assured that no covering covers them from the eye of Allah, and only remorse, shamefacedness and fear cover them. For you acquire, by their presence in your heart, the sending forth of the armies of fear and shame from there places of hiding, and your self is humbled by them, and your heart becomes lowly under the same, and you stand before Allah in the posture of a creature who is guilty and wicked, and a fugitive who has repented and returned to his Lord, bowing his head from shame and fear.

The Turning towards the *qiblah* is a turning of the outward face from other directions to the direction of the House of Allah. Do you suppose that turning the heart from there things to the matter of Allah is not desired of you? Away with you! for there is nothing else desired but it! These external activities are only settings in motion of the inward activities, a restraining of the members, and a quieting of them by the holding on to one direction, so that they may not wrong the heart. For, whenever they do wrong, and act oppressively in their movements and their turnings to their directions they desire the heart to follow, and they turn away with it from the Face of Allah. So, let the face of your heart be with the face of your body, and know that as a face does not turn toward the direction of the House except by turning away from everything else, so the heart does not turn towards Allah except by being free of all else besides. Muhammad has said, "Whenever a creature stands up for the Worship, with his inclination, his face and his heart towards Allah, he departs (from his sins[128]) innocent as he was the day his mother bore him."

128. This is an addition of Sayyid Murtada's from other versions of the tradition.

The Standing erect is only standing in person and heart before Allah. So let your head, which is your highest member, be bent, lowered and inclined, and let the placing of your head out of its erect position be an indication of the heart's grasp of humility, abasement and freedom from headship and pride. Let there be on your mind at this point the peril of standing before Allah, in dread of the place of observation, upon the presentation of your request. Know at once that you are standing before Allah, He being your Examiner. So, stand before Him as you stand before some earthly king, if you are unable to perceive the extent of His majesty. Nay more, consider, during the continuance of your standing in your Worship, that you are regarded and watched by the watchful eye of a righteous man of your family, one whom you desire to recognise you as righteous. For, upon that, your members calm down and become subdued, and all parts of you quiet down, fearful lest that miserable weak king will ascribe to you but little humility. So, whenever you feel in yourself the restraint there is under the observation of some miserable creature, chide yourself, and say to it, "You claim knowledge and love of Allah! Then are you not ashamed of your boldness toward Him, you esteem one of His creatures and fear men, without fearing Him. Who has more right that you should fear Him?" For that reason when Abu Hurairah asked, "Of what sort is shamefacedness toward Allah?" Muhammad said, "Be ashamed before Him as you are ashamed before a righteous man of your family."[129]

As for the Intention, resolve to respond to Allah by obeying His command to perform the Worship, completing it and abstaining from what[130] it prohibits and what corrupts it, and by sincerely doing all that for the Face of Allah, hoping for His reward, fearing His punishment, seeking nearness to Him, taking upon yourself His favour in His permitting you to have communion, in spite of your evil manners and your numerous disobediences. Magnify to yourself the dignity of communion with Him, and how you are communing, and with what you are communing. At that it is fitting that your brow should perspire

129. The other texts read "of your people".
130. The other texts read "defects in it".

from shame and your muscles should quiver from awe, and your face turn yellow from fear.

As for the *takbir*, the exclamation, "Allah is greater!" whenever your tongue pronounces it, it is fitting that your heart should not give it the lie. For, if there is in your heart anything greater than Allah, Allah testifies that you are a liar, even though the words be truthful, as was testified against the Hypocrites, in their saying, "Muhammad is the Messenger of Allah." For, if your inclination is more powerful than the command of Allah, you are more obedient to it than you are to Allah. Then you have adopted it as your God, and have magnified it, for it is about to happen that your saying, "Allah is greater!" is speech on your tongue alone, while your heart hangs back from assisting it. How great would be the peril in that, were it not for repentance and asking forgiveness, and thinking well of the kindness and pardon of Allah!

As for the Opening Supplication, its first words are, "I have turned my face to Him Who divided the heavens and the earth." The meaning of "face" is not the external face, for you turned it only to the direction of the *qiblah*, while Allah is far removed from the circumstance that directions should limit Him, so that you might turn towards Him by the face of your body. The face of the heart is the only thing by which you may turn to the Divider[131] of the heavens and the earth. So look to it, as to whether it is turned to its wishes, and its concerns in the house

---

131. Sayyid Murtada's note adds that the one who has knowledge of Allah says: "I turn my face (and the face of a thing is its essence and its real existence), that is, I set myself standing, as Thou hast commanded me, before the One Who divided the heavens and the earth. The thought is directed to the saying of Allah. 'Then We severed them both' (Qur'an, xx. 31); that is, the One Who differentiated my outward and my inward (being) and my unseen and my seen, and set limits between the spiritual powers in my essence, as He differentiated the heavens one from another."

Baidawi explains the Qur'an reference by saying that the heavens were one, and were divided by the different movements into the firmaments and the earths were one, and were made, by the variation of their modes of entity and their circumstances, into layers of sections.

and the bazar, following its desires, or whether it is turned the Divider of the heavens: look out for yourself, lest the first broaching of the communion be by a lie and a fabrication. The face will surely not turn toward Allah except by its turning away from all else. So strive at once to turn it to Him, and if you are unable to do it continually, let your speech, at the time, be truthful.

When you say, "Hanif,[132] Muslim,"[133] it is fitting that there should occur to your mind that the Muslim is one from whose tongue and hand Muslims are secure. If it is not so, then you are a liar. So strive to resolve upon it in the future and have repentance for previous conditions.

When you say, "I am not one of the associators," let there occur to your mind the hidden association. For, the saying of Allah, "So, let him who, hopes to meet his Lord, do good and not associate anyone else in the religious service of his Lord!" (Qur'an, xviii. 110), came down concerning anyone who seeks, by his religious service, both the Face of Allah and the praise of men. So beware, guarding against this association, and have the feeling of shame in your heart, since you have described yourself as not being among the associators without being innocent of this kind of association, for the name of "association" applies to little or much of it.

When you say, "My Worship and my devotion, my living and my dying belong to Allah," know that this is the state of one lost to himself, found to his Lord, and that if it proceed from one whose pleasure and anger, whose rising and sitting, whose desire in life and dread of death are on account of things of this life, such a one is not adapted to the state.

When you say, "I take refuge in Allah from Satan the Stoned," know that he is your enemy and is lying in wait to turn your heart away from Allah, envious of you and account of your communion with Allah, and your prostration before Him, although he was accursed on account of one prostration (to Adam[134]) which he

132. Sayyid Murtada's definition of the term is "one inclining from the false faith to the real,."
133. The Muslim is "one who keeps Muslims safe from his tongue and hand." The tradition referred to is "The Muslim is a brother of the Muslim, who does not oppress him and does not culminate him."
134. This is added by Sayyid Murtada.

abandoned and was not disposed to by Allah. And know that your seeking refuge in Allah from him is by abandoning whatever he loves and exchanging it for what Allah loves, and is not only by your saying, "I take refugé in Allah," for, when a wild beast or an enemy purposes to tear to pieces or to kill anyone, and the latter says, "I take refuge from you in this strong fortress," while remaining in his place, that does not benefit him. Rather, nothing rescues him but the changing of place. Likewise, the words only will not do any good to him who follows the desires, which are the things liked of Satan, and disliked of the Compassionate One. So let him unite the words with the resolve of taking refuge in the fortress of Allah from the evil of Satan. His fortress is, "There is no god but Allah!" since Allah[135] said, in something which our Prophet related, "There is not god but Allah' is My fortress, and whoever enters My fortress is safe from My punishment." The one guarded in it is the one who has no object of worship but Allah. But the one who adopts his inclination as his god is in the open field of Satan, not in the fortress of Allah.

Know that his device is to engage you in your Worship with thinking of the next abode and the method of carrying out benevolences, in order to prevent you from understanding what you are reciting. So, know that all that diverts you from understanding the meaning of your Recital is evil suggestion (from Satan[136]), for the movement of your tongue is not what is intended, but rather, what is intended is the meaning.

As regards the Recital, there are three kinds of people: (a) the man who moves his tongue while his heart is unmindful; (b) the man who moves his tongue with his heart following his tongue, so that he hears and understands from it, as if he heard it from someone else, this being the degree of those who will be on the right hand; and (c) the man whose heart goes ahead to the meanings first, and then the tongue serves the heart and interprets it, for there is a difference between having the tongue as the interpreter of the heart and the teacher of it, while "those who are drawn near"[137] are those whose tongues interpret their hearts,

135. Sayyid Murtada supplies this subject.
136. This is added from Sayyid Murtada.
137. The allusion is to Qur'an, lvi. 11-12.

and whose hearts are not followers of their tongues.

Further, the detailed interpretation of the inner realities is that, when you say, "In the name of Allah the Merciful and Compassionate," you intend by it the seeking of the blessing for the beginning of the Recital of the speech of Allah; Understand that its meaning is that all matters are by (the act of) Allah, and that what is meant by "the name" here is "the One named," and, if the affairs are by Allah, assuredly the praise is Allah's. The meaning of "the praise" is that thanks belong to Allah, since favours are all from Allah. Whoever thinks any favour is from any other than Allah, or has in mind, by his thinking, someone else besides Allah, not realising that any other is a benefactor because he is made subservient by Allah, is defective in his saying the *basmalah* and the Praise according to the measure of his turning to anyone besides Allah.

So, when you say, "the Merciful and Compassionate," let there be present in your heart the kinds of His favours, that His mercy may be evident to you, and your hope may be raised by it. Next, stir up from your heart, magnifying and fear, by saying, "Possessor of the Day of Judgment"--magnifying, because there is no right of possession that is not His, and fear, because of the dread of the Day of Recompense and Accounting, of which He is Possessor. Then renew the singleness of your devotion by saying, "To Thee do we render the service of slaves," and renew the sense of inability, of need and of being devoid of power and strength, by saying, "Of Thee we ask aid." Be assured that your obedience was made easy only by His aid, that His was the gift, since He helped you to obey Him, and employed you for His religious service, and made you worthy for communion with Him, for, if He had forbidden you His assistance, you would be one of the outcasts, along with Satan the Cursed.

Next, when you finish the Seeking Refuge and saying the *basmalah* and the Praise, and (expressing[138]) that you need help absolutely, specify your request, but do not request anything but your most important needs, and say, "Guide us into the Straight Road, which leads to Thy vicinity, and brings us to Thy pleasure!"

---

138. This is in the other texts.

Add to this explanation and detail, with emphasis, calling to witness those of the prophets, saints, martyrs and righteous, upon whom He poured out the favour of guidance, rather than of the unbelievers and those of the Jews and Christians and Sabeans who turned aside, with whom He was angry.

Next, beg for an affirmative answer, and say, "*Amin*!" for, when you recite the Fatihah so, you are like one of those of whom Allah said, in that about which the Prophet told us, "The Worship is divided between Me and My creature into two halves, one half to Me and one half to My creature. (My creature has what he asked.[139]). The creature says, 'Praise belongs to Allah, the Lord of the worlds', and Allah says, "Allah hears whoever says His praise. My creature has said My praise and My eulogy."' That is the meaning of His saying, 'Allah hears whoever says His praise," and so on.

Did you not have from your Worship any good fortune except Allah's remembrance of you, in His majesty and greatness, that would suffice you as a prize. Do you ask, "How so?" Because of what you may hope for of reward and kindness from Him.

Likewise it is fitting that you should understand what you recite from the *surahs*, as shall appear in the Book of the Recital of the Qur'an, so that you may not be unmindful of His command, of His prohibition, promise, threat, or warning, and of the stories of His prophets in the Qur'an, and mention of His gifts and His goodness. To everyone there is a right, Hope is the right of a promise. Fear is the right of a threat. Determination is the right of a command and a prohibition. Taking warning is the right of admonition. Thankfulness is the right of the mention of a favour. Taking a lesson is the right of the stores of the prophets.

It is related that when Zurarah b. Ufi[140] reached the saying of Allah, "So, when the trumpet is blown" (Qur'an, lxxiv. 8) he fell down dead.

---

139. Sayyid Murtada omits this from his text, but it quotes it in his comment.

140. Zurarah b. Ufi al-'Amiri al-Harathi al-Basri (Abu Hajib) Successor Judge in al-Basrah (d. 93 A.H.).

Whenever Ibrahim al-Nakha'i[141] heard the words of Allah, "When the heavens split asunder" (Qur'an, lxxxiv. 81), he was so troubled that his limbs knocked together.

'Abdallah b. Waqid[142] said, "I saw Ibn 'Umar worship with the appearance of one fried."[143] He had a right to have his heart burn at the promise and threatening of his Lord, since he was a guilty and humble creature before an overpowering Tyrant.[144]

These inner realities exist according to the degrees of understanding. The understanding is according to the greatness of the knowledge and the purity of the heart, and the degrees of that are not limited. The Worship is the key of the hearts, in which the secrets of the words are revealed.

So this is the right belonging to the Recital, and it is the right of the Invocations and of the Praises also.

Next he observes awe in his Recital, for he recites with distinctness, without haste, for that makes meditation easier. He also makes a distinction between the tones in verses of mercy and of punishment, of primise and threat, of praise, magnifying and glorifying. Al-Nakha'i,[145] whenever he passed over anything like the saying of Allah, "Allah has not adopted any son" (Qur'an, xxiii 93), and "There is no deity along with Him" (cf. Qur'an, xxvii. 61-65), used to lower the voice, as one ashamed to make mention of Him by means of anything (not befitting Him[146]). It is related that it used to be said to a reciter of the Qur'an, "Recite, pronounce elegantly and read distinctly, as you were accustomed to recite distinctly in the world."

---

141. Sayyid Murtada says that others say it was not Ibrahim al-Nakha'i (see above, Chapter 1, note 27) but Ibrahim b. Adham b. Mansur b. Yazid b. Jabir (Abu Ishaq) al-Tamimi al-'Ijli, famous ascetic of Balkh (d. 160-68 A.H.).
142. 'Abdallah b. Waqidi b. 'Abdallah b. 'Umar b. al-Khattab, al-Qarashi al-'Adwai al-Madani (d. 119 A.H.).
143. The 1334 text has "overcome".
144. This is one of the names of Allah, Qur'an lix. 23.
145. Sayyid Murtada says this is probably Ibrahim al-Nakha'i, but may be his maternal uncle (Chapter 1, note 27).
146. This is omitted from Sayyid Murtada's text.

The continuance of the Standing Posture is a reminder of the setting up of the heart with Allah, according to one description of presence. Muhammad said, "Allah receives the worshipper kindly as long as he does not turn away." As it is obligatory to guard the head and the eye from turning to different directions, so likewise it is obligatory to guard the heart from turning to anything else than the Worship. So, whenever it turns to anything else than Him, remind it of the gazing of Allah upon you, and of the unseemliness of treating lightly the One Who is communed with, when the one who is communing is unmindful, so that it should return to it (the Worship[147]). Impose humbleness upon the heart, for freedom from turning away, inwardly and outwardly, is the fruit of humbleness. Whenever the inward is humble, the outward is humble. Muhammad, seeing a man at Worship playing with his beard, said, "As for this one, were his heart humble, his members would be." For the flock is under the rule of the shepherd, and for this reason it is set forth in supplication, "O Allah, restore the shepherd and the flock!" that is, the heart and the other members.

Abu Bakr al-Siddiq, in his Worship, used to be as if he were a tent-stake, and Ibn al-Zubair[148] used to be as if he were wood. A certain one of them used to be quiet in his prostration to such an extent that sparrows alighted on him as if he were inanimate. All that is what the natural disposition requires before one of the sons of the earth who is to be magnified, so how shall it not demand it before the King of kings in the case of anyone who has experiential knowledge of the King of kings? Everyone who is composed submissively before any other than Allah, while, as a trifler, his extremities are restless before Allah, does that because of deficiency of knowledge of the majesty of Allah, and of His gazing upon his heart and his conscience.

'Ikrimah[149] said about the saying of Allah, "Who sees you when you stand up, and your turning over among those prostrating"

---

147. This is Sayyid Murtada's interpretation. Some texts read hu, which would refer to Allah.

148. 'Abdallah b. al-Zubair, Quraishite general, cousin of the Prophet d. 72 A.H.).

149. Abu 'Abdallah 'Ikrimah, manumitted slave of Ibn 'Abbas, Successor (d. 105 A.H.; and it is said, 106 and 107 A.H.).

(Qur'an, xxvi. 18, 19), that this meant his (i.e., Muhammad's[150]) standing up, his bowing, prostrating and sitting.

At the Bowing and Prostration it is fitting that you renew the remembrance of the mightiness of Allah, and that you raise your hands, seeking protection in the pardon of Allah from His punishment, by the renewal of intention, following the usage of His Prophet. Next, make a fresh beginning for Him, as to lowliness and humbleness, in your Bowing, and strive to move your heart, and renew your humbleness, and you should feel that, as well as the might of your Lord, together with your own lowliness and the highness of Your Lord. You seek aid in establishing that in your heart by means of your tongue. Then you say the praise of your Lord and bear witness to Him of His greatness, and say, "O the praise of my great Lord!" and, "He is greater than every great one!" Reiterate that in your heart, that you may confirm it by your reiteration.

Next, you rise from your Bowing, hoping that He may be a Merciful One to you, and confirming the hope in your self by saying, "Allah hears whoever says His praise," that is, answers whoever thanks Him.

Next, you follow that with thanksgiving which is demanded as additional, and you say, "O our Lord, Thine is the praise," and you increase the praise by saying, "To the fulness of heavens and the fulness of the earth."

Next you bend down for the Prostration, which is the highest degree of submission, for the dearest of your members, which is your face, gets hold of the humblest thing, which is the dust. If it is possible for you not to put any obstruction between them, so that your prostrate on the ground, do so, for it produces greater humbleness and is more conducive to lowliness. Whenever you place yourself in the place of lowliness, know that you have placed it in its proper place, and have returned the branch to the trunk, for of the dust were you formed and to it you return.[151]

So, at this, renew to your heart the remembrance of the greatness of Allah, and say, "O the praise of my Lord, Most High!"

150. This is Sayyid Murtada's addition.
151. The reference is to Qur'an, xx. 57.

and confirm it by many repetitions, for one repetition is of weak effect. Then, when your heart is moved, and that is evident, let your hope find assurance in the mercy of Allah, for His mercy makes haste towards weakness and lowliness, and not towards pride and conceit.

Then raise your head, say the *takbir* and request what you need, saying, "O Lord, forgive and have mercy, and pass over what Thou knowest," or whatever supplication you wish. Then strengthen your humility by repetition and then return to the Prostration a second time.

As for the Witnessing, when you sit down for it, sit down in a proper manner, and state that all the performances of the Worship and good things, i.e. pure dispositions by which you seek access, are Allah's and likewise the dominion is Allah's, this being the meaning of the *tahiyat,* Greetings. Then cause the Prophet to be present to your heart, and also his noble personality and say, "Peace be upon you, O Prophet, and the mercy and blessing of Allah!" Let your expectation be firm that it will reach him, and that will return to you one more perfect than it.

Next, salute yourself and the righteous creatures of Allah. Then consider that Allah will return to you a perfect Salutation, according to the number of His righteous creatures.

Next, bear witness to Allah of His oneness, and to Muhammad, His Prophet, of his mission, renewing the covenant of Allah, by repeating the two words of the witness,[152] beginning anew to seek protection in it.

Then make your Supplication at the end of your Worship in the words of the traditional supplication, with humbleness, submissiveness, imploration and true hope of an answer. Associate in your supplication your parents and the rest of the Muslims.

In the Salutation have in mind a salutation upon the angels and those present, and have the Intention of closing the Worship by it. Then have the sense of thankfulness to Allah for His assistance in the completion of this obedience, and imagine to yourself that you are taking leave of this Worship of yours, and that you perhaps may not live for another like it.

---

152. These are the two parts of the Muslim testimony.

Muhammad said to the one he commanded, "Make your Worship a leave-taking Worship."

Then make your heart feel caution and shame on account of your deficiency in the Worship. Fear that your Worship may not be accepted and that you are hated on account of some guilt, outward and inward, and your Worship will be returned to your face. Yet, for all that, hope that He will accept it, through His generosity and favour. Yahya b. Waththab,[153] whenever he worshipped, used to wait as long a while as it pleased Allah, with the pain of the Worship evident upon him. Ibrahim al-Nakah'i used to remain after the Worship for a while, as if he were ill.

This is the detailed description of the Worship of the humble, "Those who in their Worship are humble" (Qur'an, vi. 92; lxx. 34) and "Those who in their Worship are persistent" (Qur'an, lxx. 23), and who commune with Allah as much as they are able in their relationship as slaves.[154]

So, let a man apply himself to these performances of the Worship. It is fitting for him to rejoice in proportion to the amount of them which was made easy for him by Allah, and, in proportion to the amount that escapes him, it is fitting for him to grieve. In his attending to this he should be energetic.

As for the Worship of the unmindful, it is perilous, unless Allah cover the failing with His mercy, but His mercy is wide and His generosity overflowing. So we ask Allah to cover us over with His mercy, and submerge us in His forgiveness, since we have no means of gaining access except confession of inability to perform obedience to Him. Know that keeping the Worship free from faults, and devoting it solely to the Face of Allah, and the payment of it in accordance with the inward Stipulations which we have mentioned of humbleness, magnifying and shame, are the cause of securing illuminations in the heart. These illuminations become keys of the unveiled knowledges. The intimates of Allah are those to whom is revealed the unseen world of the heavens and the earth. The Divine secrets are unveiled only

153. Yahya b. Waththab al-Asadi, Kufi, a most excellent reciter (d. 103 A.H.).

154. The term here is *'ubudiyah.*

in the Worship, and particularly in the Prostration. For that reason Allah said, "And prostrate yourselves and draw near" (Qur'an, xcvi. 19).

The unveiling every worshipper receives is only according to the measure of his freedom from the troublings of this life. That varies in strength and weakness, in littleness and greatness, in clearness and obscurity, so that there is disclosed to some the thing itself, and the thing is disclosed to others in a likeness of it, just as this life[155] is disclosed to some as a carcass with Satan, in the form of a dog, crouched upon it, calling upon it [and calling men to it[156]].

There is difference also as to what the unveiling consists in, for to some are revealed certain of the qualities and majesty of Allah, and to another, some of His deeds, and to another, particulars of the sciences[157] of practical religion. There are, to distinguish these inner realities, at all times, hidden means, without number. Of these the strongest is suitable solicitude, for, whenever it is turned to some specified thing, that is the first to be unveiled. Since these are not reflected except in a polished mirror, when the mirror is altogether rust coloured, guidance is veiled from it, not on account of stinginess on the part of the One Who bestows guidance, but rather on account of the evil of the rust accumulated upon the place where the guidance is given.

Tongues are hasty in denying anything like that, since the natural disposition is so constituted that it denies what is not present. Had the unborn child intelligence, it would deny the

---

155. "Life here is one of the metaphysical qualities," explains Sayyid Murtada.
156. This clause is an addition of Sayyid Murtada's.
157. Knowledge pertaining to the next abode is of two kinds, *'ilm al-mu'dmalah* and *'ilm al-mukashafah.* The former is the science of practical religion, including questions of faith, ethics and canon law, including such duties as are incumbent on him on recurring occasions, such as the duties of the Worship, Fasting, etc. The knowledge of the Unveiled is an expression for the light that appears in the heart after its purification and reveals the inner and spiritual meanings and realities. The definitions of them are in the Book of Knowledge, the first of the *Ihya'* (Sayyid Murtada, I, 162 ff.).

possibility of the existence of man in the expanse of the air. Had a child any power of differentiation at all, it would perhaps deny what the intelligent claim to apprehend of the unseen world of the heavens and the earth. In like manner, man in every state is on the point of denying what is beyond him. Whoever denies saintship must necessarily deny prophetship. Mankind was formed to be of all sorts, so no one should deny what is beyond his degree. Yea, some, since they sought this state on account of a disputatious and confusing discussion, and did not seek it on account of a clearing of the heart of all things other than Allah, missed it, and so they denied its existence. Now, whoever does not belong to the people of unveiling must at least believe in the Unseen, and acknowledge belief in it until he sees by experience. For, in Tradition it is said, "Whenever a creature stands up for the Worship, Allah raises the veil between Himself and His creature, and meets him face to face, and angels from before his shoulders to the firmament stand worshipping with his Worship and say, *'Amin'* to his supplication, while righteousness from the clouds of the sky is rained upon the worshipper into the parting of his hair, and a crier calls out, 'Did this communing one know the One he is communing with, he would not turn, and the doors of heaven are open to those who worship--and Allah makes His creature who worships Him excel His angels in beauty."

Now, the opening of the door of heaven and the meeting of Allah with him face to face are a metaphor for the unveiling which were have mentioned. In the *Tawrah* it is written, "O son of Adam, do not lack strength for standing before Me as a worshipper, weeping, for I am Allah, Who drew near to you, and in the unseen world you saw My light!" Someone said, "We used to think that weakness and weeping and the unexpected attainment of unveiling which the worshipper finds in his heart are from the nearness of the Lord to his heart." If this nearness is not nearness in location, it has no other meaning than nearness of guidance and mercy and uncovering of the veil.

It is said, "When the worshipper performs two *rak'ahs,* ten rows of angels marvel at him, each row having ten thousand, and Allah makes him excel a hundred thousand angels. That is because the creature has brought together in the Worship the Standing Posture, the Sitting, Bowing and Prostration, while Allah has distributed that upon forty thousand angels, for, those who stand do not bow until Resurrection Day, and those who prostrate do not stand until Resurrection Day, and likewise those who bow and those who sit." For, whatever nearness and rank Allah has apportioned to the angels is inseparably connected with them, continuing in one state which does not increase or decrease. For that reason Allah has stated about them, that they said, "And there is no one of us but has a certain position" (Qur'an, xxxvii. 164).

A Man is distinguished from the angels in his ascent from one degree to another for "He does not cease to draw near to Allah." He has the advantage of nearness and increase of it, since the door of increase is closed to the angels. Each one has only the rank which is his endowment, and the religious service in which he is engaged. He does not change over to anything else and is not remiss in it. So they do not esteem themselves too great for His Worship, and do not tire uttering praises: by night and by day they are not remiss.[158]

The key of increase of the degrees is the performances of the Worship. Allah said, "Those believers have prospered who in their Worship are humble!" (Qur'an, xxiii. 1-2). So He praised them, after referring to their faith by mentioning Worship which is united with humbleness. Then He sealed the qualities of those who prosper by the Worship, also saying, "And those who in their Worship are persevering" (Qur'an, xxiii. 9). Then He said, regarding the fruit of these qualities, "Those are the inheritors, who inherit paradise, in which they remain eternally" (Qur'an, xxiii. 10-11). So He ascribed to them, prosperity at first, and then the inheritance of Paradise at the last.

I do not hold that the gabbling of the tongue, together with unmindfulness of the heart, end at this goal. For that reason Allah said, about those in the opposite condition, "What caused you to enter into the Saqar [Plane of Hell]?"[159] They said, "We were not of those who worship" (Qur'an, lxxiv. 43-44). So the worshipers are the inheritors of Paradise. They are those who see the light of Allah, and who have enjoyment in His nearness and His approach to their hearts.

158. The allusions are to Qur'an, xxi. 19-20.
159. This is Sayyid Murtada's explanation.

We ask Allah to make us to be of them, and to rescue us from the punishment of him whose words seem good and whose deeds are evil. He is the Gracious Giver, and the Ancient Doer of good.

Stories and Traditions About the Worship of the Humble

Know that humbleness is a fruit of faith and a result of the certainly consequent upon [observing] the majesty of Allah. Whoever is apportioned that, is humble in the Worship and at other time even in solitude of any kind. For the cause of humbleness is the knowledge of the gaze of Allah upon His creature, and the knowledge of His majesty and the knowledge of the creature's shortcoming. So, from the recognition of these things humbleness is born, and it is not confined to the Worship. On that account it is related about a certain one that he did not raise his head to the sky for forty years, out of shamefacedness towards Allah, and lowliness before Him.

Al-Rabi' b. Khuthaim,[160] because of his strictness in lowering his gaze and bending down his head, was thought by some to be blind. He used to go frequently to the residence of Ibn Mas'ud during twenty years, and whenever his maid-servant would see him she would say to Ibn Mas'ud, "Your blind friend has come," and Ibn Mas'ud used to laugh at her remark, And whenever he would knock on the door, the slave-girl would go out to him and then see him bending down and lowering his gaze, and Ibn Mas'ud, whenever he would look at him, used to say, " 'And bear glad tidings to those! who humble themselves!' " (Qur'an, xxii. 35). Is it not so, by Allah, that were Muhammad to see you, he would rejoice in you!" and in another variation[161] it says, "He would glorify you," and in another variation it says, "He would love you!" He walked one day with Ibn Mas'ud among the blacksmiths, and when he looked upon the forge blowing and the fires blazing he fainted and fell unconscious. Ibn Mas'ud say at his head until Worship time and he did not revive, so he carried him on his back to his residence. Thus he remained, unconscious, until the same hour [next day] in which he fainted, so that five Worship times escaped him, with Ibn Mas'ud at his head, saying, "This,

160. Al-habi' b. Khuthaim (d. 60-64 A.H.).
161. This is added by the other texts.

by Allah, is fear!"

Rabi' used to say, "I have never entered upon the Worship at all, except what concerned me in it was only what I was saying and what was being said to me."

'Amir b. 'Abdallah[162] was one of the most lowly of worshippers. and when he would worship his daughter would perhaps beat the tambourine and the women would speak of whatever they would want in the house, and he would hear that but would not understand it.

He was asked one day, "Does your self speak to you in the Worship about anything?" He replied, "Yes, about my standing before Allah, and my departure to one of the two places of abode." He was asked, "Then do you experience anything of what we experience of matters of this life?" He replied, "Indeed, that lanceheads should repeatedly pierce me is more desirable to me than that I should experience in my Worship what you experience." He used to say, "Were the veil removed I would not become more certain."

Muslim b. Yasar was also one of that kind, and we have already reported that he did not become aware of the falling of a column in the mosque while he was at the Worship.

One of the extremities of one of them was consumed by a wasting disease and required amputation, but it was not possible. So it was said, "In the Worship he does not feel anything happening," and so it was cut off while he was at the Worship.

A certain one said, "The Worship belongs to the next abode, so when you enter upon it you pass out of this life."

It was said to another, "Does your self speak about anything of this life in the Worship? He replied, "Neither in the Worship nor at other times."

A certain one was asked, "Do you recall anything in the Worship?" Then he replied, "And is anything more dear to me than the Worship, so that I should recall it in it?"

Abu al-Darda'[163] used to say, "It is an indication of a man's

162. 'Amir b. 'Abdallah b. al-Zubair (see supra, note 53).
163. Abu al-Darda' al-Khazraji al 'Ansari (d. 31 A.H.).

understanding of canon law that he attends to his need first, before his entering upon the Worship, that he may enter upon the Worship with his heart empty of care."

One of them used to do the Worship quickly, out of ear of evil suggestions.

It is related that 'Ammar b. Yasir[164] performed a Worship and did it quickly. So it was said to him, "You did it quickly, O Abu al-Yaqzan!" So he asked. "Did you see me diminish its limits any?" They replied, "No." He said, "I strove to outstrip the oversight caused by Satan."

The Messenger of Allah said, "A creature performs the Worship with not half of it, or a third or a fourth or a fifth or a sixth or a tenth, of it credited to him.

He (i.e., 'Ammar[165]) used to say, "There is credited to a creature only what he comprehends of his Worship."

It is said, "Talhah[166] and Zubair[167] and a group of the Companions with them were the quickest of men at the Worship, and they said, 'We outstrip by it the suggestion of Satan.' "

It is related that 'Umar b. al-Khattab[168] declared from the pulpit, "A man may grow white of the two sides of his beard, in Islam, without having performed for Allah a single Worship." He was asked, "And how is that?" So he replied, "He does not complete its humbleness and its lowliness and his approach to Allah in it."

Abu al-'Aliyah[169] was asked about the saying of Allah, "Those who were forgetful of their Worship" (Qur'an, cvii. 5). He replied, "It is he who is forgetful of his Worship, for he does not know how many *rakah's* he goes out from, whether an even number of

---

164. 'Ammar b. Yasir b. 'Amir b. 'Malik (Abu al-Yaqzan), partisan of 'Ali (d. 37 A.H.).
165. Sayyid Murtada adds this.
166. Talhah b. 'Ubaidallah, Companion (d. 36 A.H.).
167. Abu 'Abdallah al-Zubair b. al'Awwam al-Qarashi al-Asadi al-Madani (see supra, note 53).
168. 'Umar b. al-Khattab, the second Khalifah (d. 23 A.H.).
169. Abu al-'Aliyah, Rafi' b. Mihran al-Basri (d. 90 A.H.)

an odd." Al-Hasan said, "It is he who forgets the time of the Worship until it departs." One of them said, "It is he, who, if he performs the Worship early in its time, does not rejoice, and, if he delays it after its early time, does not grieve, for he does not consider hastening it as a benefit, or deferring it as a sin."

Know about the Worship that a part of it is reckoned and part of it is recorded without the rest, as the traditions have shown, although canon lawyers used to say, "The Worship, as regards its validity, is not divided into parts." But that has another meaning which we have mentioned.[170] This meaning the traditions have indicated, since it is related, "The deficiency of the Prescribed Worship is made up by the Supererogatory ones." In Tradition, it is said "'Is a said, 'Allah says, "By the Prescribed Worship, My creature is saved from Me, and by the Supererogatory ones My creature draws nigh to Me." '"

The Prophet said, "Allah said, 'My creature is not saved from Me except by the payment of what I prescribed upon him.' "

It is related that the Prophet performed a Worship, and omitted a verse from its recital. So, when he turned away he said, "What have I recited?" The people kept quiet, so he asked Ubayy b. Ka'b,[171] and he replied, "You recited such a *surha*, and omitted such a verse, and we do not know whether you exchanged or removed." Upon which he remarked, "You are the man, O Ubayy!" Then he advanced to the others and said, "What can people be thinking of who are present at their Worship and who complete their ranks with their Prophet before them, and do not know what he recites to them from the Book of their Lord! Did not Bani Isra'il do so, so that Allah revealed to their Prophet, 'Say to your people, "You present Me your bodies and you give Me your tongues, but you are absent from Me your hearts! Vain is what you proceed upon!" This proves that hearing and understanding what the *imam* recites is a substitute for the recital of the *surah* by oneself.

One of them said, "There is a man who performs a Prostration: according to his own thought, he has come near to

170. See Chapter 3.
171. Ubayy b. Ka'b, Helper (d. 22, or 30 A.H.).

Allah by means of it, but, were his sins in his Prostration distributed upon the inhabitants of a city, they would perish." He was asked, "And how is that?" He replied, "He is prostrating before Allah while his heart is attentive to some desire or observing some vanity that has taken possession of him."

This, then, is the description of the humble, and so these narratives and traditions, together with what has preceded, prove that the root of the Worship is humbleness and the presence of the heart, and that the movements alone, with unmindfulness, are of little profit in the Place of Return. And Allah knows better. We ask of Allah the beauty of His assistance.

4

Leadership and Example

Upon the *imam* there are duties before the Worship, during the Recital, in the Elements of the Worship and after the Salutation.

The duties which precede the Worship are six in number.

The first of them is that one should not go forward to the leadership for a people who dislike him. If they disagree, regard is to be shown to the majority. Yet, if the minority are people of benevolence and piety, regard to them is preferable. In Tradition it says, "Three there are whose Worship does not pass beyond their heads: the runaway slave, a woman whose husband is displeased with her, and an *imam* who leads a people who dislike him."

As he is prohibited from going forward by their dislike, so likewise he is prohibited from going forward if there should be behind him one who is more learned than he [or a better reciter[171]], except whenever he who would be preferable to him declines. But, if it is not his duty to refrain for reasons like these, let him go forward whenever he is first and knows that the conditions of the leadership, exist in him. In that case any refusal is disliked, for it is said, "A people one after the other refused the leadership after the Worship had begun, and the ground swallowed them up."

As for what is related of the refusal of the leadership on the part of the Companions, the reason for that was their choosing one whom they thought to be preferable for that, or, their fear, for themselves, of forgetfulness and the peril of the responsibility of their Worship, for, "The *imams* are the guarantors." It might

---

171. This phrase is additional in Sayyid Murtada's text.

be that the heart of one who was not accustomed to that position would perhaps feel anxious and that would disturb the singleness of heart desired in his Worship, because of his diffidence towards those imitating him, especially in the audible part of the Recital. So, the cautiousness of some who guarded themselves against that was on account of reasons of this sort.

The second is that, whenever a man is given the choice between giving the Call to the Worship, and the leadership, he should choose the leadership. For, each one of them has some excellence, but uniting them is disliked. Nay, rather, it is fitting that the *imam* should be other than the one who gives the Call, and, if the joining of the two offices is objectionable, the leadership is preferable. Those who say, "The Call to Worship is preferable," say so on account of what we have reported concerning the excellence of the Call to Worship, and on account of the saying of Muhammad, "The *imam* is a guarantor and the *mu'adhdhin* is a trustee." So they said, "In the leadership there is the guarantor's risk."

Muhammad said, "The *imam* is *amir,*[172] so whenever he bows, bow, and whenever he prostrates, prostrate."

In Tradition it is said, "If he completes the Worship it is credited to him and to them, and if he comes short, it is against him and not against them."

A further reason for their opinion is because Muhammad said, "O Allah, guide the *imams* and forgive the *mu'adhdhins,*" for forgiveness is preferable in an intercession, for, a request for forgiveness includes guidance.

In the Record it is said, "Whoever acts as *imam*[173] in a mosque seven years has the Garden due him without any reckoning, and one who has been a *mu'adhdhin* for forty years will enter the Garden without a reckoning". For that reason it is reported about the Companions that they used to decline the leadership, one after another, for the truth is that the leadership is more excellent, since

172. The other texts have *amin*, "trustworthy".

173. Sayyid Murtada reads "acts as *mu'adhddin*" here and in the second part of the record. The first is then evidently a misprint, as the other texts have, "acts as *imam.*"

the Messenger of Allah continued at it, as well as Abu Bakr, 'Umar and the *imams* after them. True, there is in it the peril of the responsibility, but, excellence goes with peril, just as the rank of the amirate and the khalifate is more honourable, on account of the saying of Muhammad, "A day of a just sultan is more honourable than the religious service of seventy years." Nevertheless, in it there is peril, and for that reason it is obligatory to put forward the most honourable and most learned. Muhammad has said, "Your *imams* are your intercessors," or he said, "Your envoy to Allah," so, if you wish your Worship to thrive, put forward the most excellent among you.

Someone of the Fathers said, "After the prophets there are none more honourable than the learned and after the learned there are none more honourable than the *imams,* performing the Worship. For, all these stand before Allah and His creation, one with prophesy, and another with learning, and the other with the support of the religion, which is the Worship'." This argument the Companions adduced in putting forward Abu Bakr al-Siddiq for the khalifate, since they said, "We considered, and lo! 'the Worship is the support of the religion,' and so we chose for this life of ours the one whom the Messenger of Allah preferred for our religious affairs." They did not put forward Bilal, arguing that Muhammad had preferred him for the office of *mu'adhdhin*!"

As for the matter that is related, that a man said to him, "Messenger of Allah! lead me to a work by which I may enter the Garden," he said, "Become a *mu'adhdhin!*" He replied, "I am not able." He said, "Become an *imam*!" He replied, "I am not able." Then he said, "Worship beside the *imam*!" perhaps he thought that he would not be acceptable in his leadership, since the calling to Worship was his own affair, while the leadership and their putting him forward was the affair of the congregation. Then afterwards he supposed that he had ability to achieve the leadership.

The third is that the *imam* shows regard for the times of the worshipping, for he performs the Worship at the beginnings of them--in order to please Allah. For, "The superiority of the beginning of the time over the end of it is like the superiority of the next abode over this life." Thus it is related from the Messenger of Allah. In Tradition it is said, "A creature may perform the Worship [at the end of its time[174]], and so it does not escape him, but truly, that of the beginning[175] of its time which escaped him had more benefit for him than this life and what is in it."

It is not fitting that he should delay the Worship out of expectation of a large congregation. Nay, rather, it is for him to lose no time to obtain he excellence of the first of its time, for that is more excellent than the large size of the congregation and than the lengthening of the *surah.*

It has been said. "They were accustomed, whenever two were present in the congregational Worship, not to wait for the third, and whenever four were present at a funeral, they would not await a fifth."

The Messenger of Allah had been delayed from the Dawn Worship, while they were on a journey (he was delayed only for the sake of the purification), and he was not waited for, and 'Abd al-Rahman[176] came forward and conducted the Worship with them, so that one *rak'ah* escaped the Messenger of Allah. Then Muhammad stood up and performed the *qada'*, Substitution, Worship. Then we were anxious about that, so Muhammad said, "You did well in doing that and keep on doing so."

He had been delayed at the Noon Worship, so they put forward Abu Bakr until the Messenger of Allah came, while they were still at Worship, so he stood at his side.

It is not for the *imam* to wait for the *mu'adhdhin,* and it is necessary for the *mu'adhdhin* to wait only for the *imam*, for the Institution of the Worship. So, when he comes, he should not await anyone else.

The fourth requirement is that he should act as *imam* as one sincerely seeking Allah's Face [and that which He has to give[177]], and as one paying back the "trust" of Allah, in respect of his purification and all the stipulations of his Worship.

---

174. Sayyid Murtada's text omits this clause.
175. See note 37 to next chapter.
176. 'Abd al-Rahman b. 'Awf, Quraishite (d.31 A.H.).
177. This is according to Sayyid Murtada's interpretation.

As for singleness of devotion, it means that he does not accept any reward for the Worship, for the Messenger of Allah gave an order to 'Uthman b. Abu al-'As al-Thaqafi[178] and said to him, "Select as *mu'adhdhin* one who does not take any reward for giving the Call to Worship!" For the Call to the Worship is a way to the Worship, and the Worship is better when a reward is not accepted for it. But, if he takes some sustenance from a mosque which has been entailed upon the one who has the position of *imam* of it, or from the sultan, or from individuals of the people, there should be no ruling to make it unlawful, but it is disliked, and dislike with regard to prescribed things is stronger than it is with regard to supererogatory acts. He may have a reward for persevering attendance upon the place, and for his watchfulness over the interests of the mosque, in establishing the Congregational Worship in that place, but not for the Worship itself.

As for the "trust," it is cleanness within from transgression and the great sins, and from persistence in minor sins. For, it is fitting that he who would be prepared for the office of *imam* should guard against that with his best energy, for he is as the envoy and intercessor for the people, so it is fitting that he should be the best of the people. Similarly as to cleanness outwardly, he should guard himself from uncleanness and impurity, for no one perceives that, so far as he is concerned, except himself. So, if he should recall, during the Worship, any uncleanness...he should not be ashamed, but, rather, let him take the hand of the one who is near to him and appoint him to succeed him. For the Messenger of Allah recalled a *janabah*, "greater uncleanness," during the Worship, so he appointed a successor, and bathed. Then he returned and entered into the Worship.

Sufyan[179] said, "Worship behind everyone, just and unjust, except one addicted to wine, one notorious for transgression, one disobedient to parents, one with an innovation or a runaway slave."

The fifth duty is that he should not recite the *takbir* until the

---

178. Abu 'Abdallah 'Uthman b. Abu al-'As al-Thaqafi at-Ta'ifi (d. 51 A.H.).

179. This is either Sufyan al-Thawri (note 6, previous chapter) or Abu Muhammad Sufyan b. 'Uyainah b. Abu Imran Maimun al-Hilali (d. 198 A.H.)

rows are arranged. So, let him turn to the right and the left, and, if he sees any defect, he should order it to be arranged. It is said, "They were accustomed to place themselves beside one another, shoulder to shoulder, and to place their ankles together." He does not recite the *takbir* until the *mu'adhdhin* finishes the Institution. The *mu'adhdhin* delays instituting the Worship after the Call by as long as it takes for the men to get ready for the Worship. In the Record it says, "Let the *mu'adhdhin* grant between the Call to Worship and the Institution a respite as long as an eater takes to finish his food...The reason for that is that....it is commanded that the evening meal should precede the Evening Worship, out of desire that the heart should be disengaged.

The sixth is that he should raise his voice in the single *takbirat al-ihram* and the rest of the *takbirs,* and the follower should not raise his voice except enough for himself to hear. He states the Intention to lead, in order to obtain reward. But if he should not state the Intention, his Worship would be valid, as well as the Worship of the people, if they stated the Intention of the imitation, and they obtain the reward of the imitation, while he does not obtain the reward of the leadership. Let them delay their *takbir* after the *takbir* of the *imam,* and begin after he has finished. And Allah knows better.

The duties of the Recital are three in number.

The first of them is that he should recite the Opening Supplication inaudibly, and likewise the Seeking Refuge, as does one worshipping alone. He utters audibly the Fatihah and the *surah* after it in both *rak'ahs* of the Morning Worship, and in the first two *rak'ahs* of both the Evening and the Sunset Worships. So also the one who worship alone. He utters audibly the *amin* in the audible Worship, as does the follower. The follower says his *amin* is unison with the *amin,* of the *imam,* not afterwards. He utters audibly the words, "In the name of Allah the Merciful and Compassionate One." The Records about it are contradictory, and the preference of al-Shafi'i[180] is for saying it audibly.

The second is that the *imam* should make three pauses in the Standing Posture, and so Samurah b. Jundub[181] and 'Imran b.

---

180. Muhammad b. Idris al-Shafi'i al-Hijazi.
181. Abu Sa'id Samurah b. Jundub, Companion (d. 58 A.H.)

al-Hasin[182] record, from the Messenger of Allah. The first of them is when he says the *takbir,* and it is the longest of them, long enough for one who is behind him to recite the Fatihah of the Book. That is the time for his reciting the Opening supplication of the Worship. For, if he should not pause, they would not be able to hear his recital and then whatever is short in their Worship would be recorded against him. But if he should pause and they should not recite the Fatihah during his pause, or should be occupied with something else, that would be against them and not against him. The second pause is when he finishes the Fatihah, in order that the one who did not recite the Fatihah in the first pause may finish his Fatihah. This is half the time of the first pause. The third pause is when he finishes the *surah,* before he bows. It is the briefest of them, and that is as long a time as separates the Recital from the *takbir,* for there is a prohibition against bringing them together.

The follower does not recite after the *imam* anything but the Fatihah. But if the *imam* does not pause, he recites the Fatihah of the Book with him, and the one who is remiss is the *imam.* If the follower should not hear the Recital of the *imam* in the audible Worship on account of his distance, or if he should be engaged in the inaudible Worship, there is no objection to the recital of the *surah* along with the Fatihah.

The third duty is that he should recite in the Morning Worship two *surahs* from the *mathani* which are less than a hundred verses. For, to be lengthy in the Recital of the Dawn Worship and to perform it before daybreak are *sunan,* Usages, but to finish it in the clear dawn does not harm one.

There is no objection if he recite in the second of the two *rak'ahs* of the Morning the latter parts of the *surahs* from the thirtieth or the twentieth verses until he finish them, for they are not repeated upon the hearing often, and so are more effective in admonition, and summon better to meditation. Some of the *'ulama',* "learned," have expressed dislike for the recital of only some of the first part of the *surah* and then breaking it off. But

182. 'Imran b. Hasin b. 'Ubaid b. Khalaf, Companion, Qadi in al-Basrah (d. 52 A.H.)

it has been related that Muhammad recited part of the *surah* of Yunus (x) and after he had completed it to the mention of Moses and Pharaoh (verses 76 to 84), he broke off and did the Bowing.

It is related that Muhammad recited in the Dawn Worship a verse from "The Cow" (ii) which was His saying, "say, We believe in Allah and what He sent down to us" (verse 130), and in the second *rak'ah*, "O our Lord! we have believed in what Thou didst send down" (iii. 46).

He heard Bilal recite from nere and there. So he asked him about that, and he replied, "I mingle the pleasant with the pleasant." So he remarked, 'You have done well."

The *imam* recites at the Noon Worship the long *surahs* of the *mufassal,* up to thirty verses, and in the Afternoon Worship half of that, and in the Sunset Worship the latter parts of the *mufassal.* The last Worship of the Messenger of Allah was the Sunset Worship. In it he recited the *surah,*. "The Sent Ones" (lxxvii,). He did not perform a Worship after that before he was taken.

On the whole, to do it quickly is preferable, especially when the congregation is large. Muhammad said concerning this concession, "When one of you leads the Worship with the people, let him do it quickly, for among them are the weak and the aged and those who have a need. When he worships by himself, let him be as long as he likes." It happened that Mu'adh b. Jabal was worshipping with some people at the evening time, and he recited "The Cow" (ii), and a man went out from the Worship and finished by himself. So they said, "The man has become a hypocrite." Then they both brought counter charges before the Messenger of Allah. So the Messenger of Allah chided Mu'adh and said, "Are you a disturber, Mu'adh? Recite the *surah* of 'Praise' (lxxxvii.), and 'The Skies and the Night-traveller' (lxxxvi.), and "The Sun and Its Morning Brightness' (xci.)."

The duties respecting the Prescribed Elements are three in number.

The first is that he does the Bowing quickly and also the Prostration, and does not increase the number of the Praises over three. For it is related from Anas that he said, "I have not seen anyone more quick as regards the Worship than the Messenger of Allah, and, at the same time, complete." It is true that it is related also that Anas b. Malik, when he worshipped behind 'Umar b. 'Abd al-'Aziz, when he was Amir in Medina, said, "Indeed, I have not worshipped behind anyone whose Worship is more like the Worship of the Messenger of Allah than that of this young man." He said, "We used to say the Praise behind him by tens." It is related inclusively that they said, "We used to recite the Praise behind the Messenger of Allah in the Bowing and the Prostration by tens." And that is excellent. But three, when the congregation is large, is better. But when there are none present but those devoted to religion there is no harm in the ten repetitions. This is the way to combine the narratives. It is fitting that the *imam* should say, at the raising of his head from the Prostration, "Allah hears whoever says He is praise."

The second duty concerns the follower. It is fitting that he should not bow and prostrate along with the *imam*. Rather, he should delay. So he does not bend for the Prostration until the forehead of the *imam* reaches the place of prostration. Such was the practice of the Companions with the Messenger of Allah. He does not bend for the Bowing until the *imam* completes his Bowing. It is said, "Men leave the Worship in three divisions: One party have twenty-five Worships, and they are those who say the *takbir* and bow after the *imam*. Another party has one Worship, and they are those who keep up with him. Another party has no Worship and they are those who go ahead of the *imam*.

There is disagreement as to whether the *imam*, in the Bowing, should wait until one coming in joins in and overtakes that *rak'ah*, in order that he may obtain the reward of worshipping with the congregation. Perhaps the preferable opinion is that that is without harm, if singleness of devotion is preserved, whenever no noticeable interval becomes apparent to those present, for their rights is to be regarded, in desisting from the lengthening of the service for them.

The third duty is that he does not increase in the Supplication of the Witnessing beyond the amount given to the Witnessing itself, guarding against being too long, and he does not include only himself in the Supplication, but rather uses the form of the plural, and says, "O Allah, forgive us!" and does not say, "Forgive me". For it is disliked in an *imam* to include only himself. There is no harm in his use of the Invocation of the protection of Allah in the Witnessing, using the five phrases transmitted from the Messenger of Allah. So he says, "We take refuge in Thee from the punishment of Hell and the punishment of the grave, and we take refuge in Thee from the testing[183] of life and death, and from the testing of the Antichrist and, whenever Thou willest testing a people, take us to Thyself without our being tested." It is said, "He is called *masih*, 'rubber,' because he rubs upon the earth in all its length," and it is said. "He is called *masih*, 'one-eyed,' because he is smooth of one eye, i.e. blind in it."

The duties of the finishing of the Worship are three in number.

The first is that he have the Intention, in the two Salutations,[184] of salutation upon the people and the angels.

The second ins that he remain stationary after the Salutation. So did the Messenger of Allah, Abu Bakr and 'Umar. He performs the *nafl*, Supererogatory, Worship in another place. But if there are women behind him he does not rise until they depart.

In the *mashhur*,[185] "well known," record it is stated that Muhammad was not accustomed to remain sitting more than long enough for him to say, "O Allah! thou art the Peace,[186] and from Thee comes peace! Thou art blessed in and of Thyself, O Possessor of majesty and honour!"

The third is that when he springs up it is fitting that he should turn his face toward the people. It is disliked for the follower to get up before the turning of the *imam*. For it is related about Talhah and Zubair that they worshipped behind an *imam*, and, after they had said the Salutation, they said to the *imam*, "How excellent was your performance of the Worship, and how complete it was, except for one thing!--after you said the Salutation you

---

183. On the word *fitnah*, cf. Baidawi, on Qur'an ii.96.
184. That is, upon the right and the left, says Sayyid Murtada.
185. Sayyid Murtada says, the word *mashhur*," "well known" is not used here in its technical sense.
186. Al-Salam, "Peace". This is one of the most beautiful names of Allah and occurs in the Qur'an only at lix. 23.

did not turn your face to the congregation." Then they said to the people, "How excellent was your Worship, only you withdrew from it before your *imam* turned."

Then the *imam* departs, whither he will, to his right or left, the right being more liked.

This is the duty of the performances of the Worship.

With regard to the Morning Worship, the *imam* adds to it the *qunut*, Supplication, and says, "O Allah, guide us!" and does not say, "Guide me." The follower says, "*Amin*!" When he reaches the words, "Thou dost judge, and art not judged!" the saying of the *amin*! is not fitting, since it is praise, so he recites it with him. He says what the *imam* says, or he *says*, "Yes indeed! and to that I am one of the witnesses," or, "You have spoken truly and done right," or some similar expression.

There is related a tradition for the raising of the two hands in the *qunut*, Supplication, and, if the tradition is valid, that is preferable, although it is different from the Supplications at the end of the Witnessing, since the hands[187] are not raised on account of them on that occasion, but reliance is to be placed on explicit statement.[188] Between the two there is also a great difference, that being that the hands have a duty in the Witnessing, and have to be placed on the things in a special form. They have no duty here, so it is not strange that the raising of the hands should be a duty in the *qunut*, Supplications, for it is fitting in supplication. And Allah knows better.

This is the whole duty of the proper manner of performing the example and the leadership. And Allah is the Helper!.

---

187. The other texts read "he does not raise his hand."

188. The use of the technical term *al-tawqifiyah* is explained in *Tuhfat al-Murid 'ala Jawharat al-Tawhid*, by al-Bajuri (Cairo, 1324 A.H.), where he says: "*Al-tawqifiyah*, that is, the possibility of the application of names to Allah depends upon their appearance in a book, or in a 'sound' or 'beautiful" *sunnah*, 'tradition,' or in an 'agreement'." In the *Qamus* (III. 199) *twaqif* in Traditon means "explanation," and in law means "a definite statement" (*nass*).

5

The Excellence of the Friday Observance: Its Properties Usages and Stipulation

Know that this is a great day, by which Allah has magnified Islam and by which He has given distinction to the Muslims. Allah said, "When there is a call to Worship on Friday, hasten to the remembrance of Allah, and cease selling" (Qur'an, lxii. 9). So, being busy in affairs of this life and in all that hinders from hastening to the Friday Observation was made unlawful.

Muhammad said, "Allah prescribed the Friday Observance upon you in this my day and in this my position." He said, "Whoever abandons the Friday Observance thrice without excuse has Allah put a seal upon his hear,"[189] and, in another version, "has thrown Islam behind his back".

A man kept returning to Ibn 'Abbas, asking him about a man who died without being accustomed to being present at the Friday Observance or a Congregational Worship. So he said, "He is in the Fire." But he did not cease returning to him monthly about that, and he would say, "He is in the Fire."

In Tradition it is said, "The People of the Two Books[190] were given Friday, and they disagreed about it and departed from it, and Allah guided us to it, and kept it back for this people and made it a feast-day for them, they being the people worthiest of

---

189. Sayyid Murtada explains: "Puts a veil upon it, so that he does not understand, and prevents him from obedience." The allusion is to the Qur'an, iv. 154, and similar passages.

190. They are the Jews and Christians.

it, in the matter of precedence, while the People of the Two Books follow after them."

In the tradition of Anas from the Prophet it is related that he said, "Gabriel[191] brought me in his palm a white mirror and said, 'This is the Friday Observance: your Lord prescribes it upon you to be a feast-day to you and to your people after you.' I said, 'And what is there for us in it?' He said. 'There is for you "the best hour," in which, whoever makes a supplication for a good that has been apportioned to him, has it given to him by Allah, or, if it be not apportioned to him, has stored up for him something greater than it; or else, he escapes from an evil decreed upon him, unless Allah protects him from a greater evil. It is the "lord of the days" among us, and we call it, in the next abode, "the day of increase". I asked, 'Why?' He said, 'Your Lord chose in the Garden a valley more odourous than white musk, so, when Friday comes, He descends from the highest heaven upon His throne, and reveals Himself to them so that they look upon His Generous Face.'"

Muhammad said. "The best day the sun shines upon is Friday. On it Adam was formed; on it he was introduced into the Garden and on it he was cast down to the earth; on it he was forgiven and on it he died; on it the Resurrection Hour will come, and it is with Allah, thc 'day of increase', So the angels name it in heaven, and it is the day for seeing Allah, in the Garden."

It is said in Tradition, "Allah has on every Friday six hundred thousand freed from the Fire."

In the tradition of Anas it is recorded that Muhammad said, "Whenever Friday is safe,[192] all the days are safe."

Muhammad said, "Hell-fire is kindled every day before the passing of the meridian, at the sun's standing balanced in the heart of the sky, so do not perform the Worship at that hour, except on Friday, for it is a Worship itself, all of it, and Hell is not kindled on that day."

---

191. For the eight different spellings of this name, see Baidawi, on Qur'an ii. 191.
192. Sayyid Murtada adds: "From the occurrence of sins in it."

Ka'b[193] said, "Allah gave preference, among cities, to Mecca, and, among the months, to Ramadan, and, among the days, to Friday, and, among the nights, to the Night of Decree."

It is said, "The birds and the serpents meet each other on Friday and say, 'Peace, peace, a goodly day!'"

Muhammad said, "Whoever dies on Friday, or on the eve of Friday, has Allah decreed for him the reward of a martyr and preservation from the testing of the grave."

Exposition of the Stipulations of the Friday Observance

Know that it shares the Stipulations of all the performances of the Worship, and is differentiated from them by six additional Stipulations.

The first is the time. If the Salutation of the *imam* occurs within the time of *'asr*, "mid-afternoon," the Friday Observance has escaped, and it is incumbent upon him to complete it as an ordinary Noon Worship of four *rak'ahs*. There is disagreement about the man who is late, when his last *rak'ah* falls after the time.

The second is the locality. It is not valid to celebrate the Friday Observance in the deserts, or on the plains, or among the tents, but it must be in a space containing buildings that are not moveable and that can contain forty of those upon whom the Friday Observance is incumbent. In this matter a village is like a town. The presence of the sultan at it is not stipulated, but it is preferable to ask his permission.

The third is the number. It is not confirmed as a valid Friday Observance with less than forty males, responsible, free, and domiciled, i.e. who do not move away from it winter or summer. Then, if they disperse, so that the number comes short, either in the time of the address or the Worship, that Friday Observance is not valid. Rather there is need of them from the first of the last.

The fourth is the congregation. Were forty in a village or a town to worship in different parties, their Friday Observance would not be valid. But a late-comer, whenever he is in time for

193. Abu Ishaq Ka'b b. Mani, al-Himyari al-Ahbar (al-Habr), (d. 32 A.H.).

the second *rak'ah* [with the *imam*[194]] overtakes the Friday Observance, and it is allowable for him to perform the second *rak'ah* by himself. But, if he does not overtake the Bowing of the *imam* in the second *rak'ah,* he does not overtake the Friday Observance, so he follows the *imam,* but he states the Intention to perform the Noon Worship and when the *imam* says the Salutation, he stands and completes it as a Noon Worship.

The fifth is that the Friday Observance should not be preceded by any other in that town. If their meeting together in one congregational mosque should be impossible, it is allowable to meet in two or three or four, according to the need. If there should be no need, the valid one is the Friday Observance in which the Opening *takbir* occurred first. When the need is a proved one, the more excellent is the Worship behind the more excellent of the two *imams.* If they are on a parity, then in the older mosque, and if they are on a parity, then in the nearer one. The largeness of the number of the men has an excellence that should be considered.

The sixth is the two addresses, which are both Prescribed, Standing up during the address is a Prescribed act, and sitting down between them is a Prescribed act. In the first there are four Prescribed parts: the Praising, the minimum of it being "Praise belongs to Allah". The second is the Blessing upon the Prophet. The third is the Command of fear towards Allah. The fourth is the Recital of a verse from the Qur'an. Likewise, the Prescribed parts of the second address are four in number except that in it the Supplication is obligatory instead of the Recital. The hearing of the two addresses is obligatory upon the forty.

The Usages

When the sun passes the meridian and the *mu'adhdhin* gives the Call and the *imam* sits on the pulpit, the individual Worship stops, except for the Worship of Greeting upon entering the mosque. Talking need not stop until the opening of the address. The speaker, *khatib,* salutes the people when he turns his face toward them and they return the Salutation. Then when the *mu'adhdhin* finishes the Call, he rises, facing the people. He does

194. This is added by Sayyid Murtada.

not turn to the right or left, but occupies his hands with the hilt of the sword or staff, and with the pulplit, in order that he may not play with his hands, or place one of them on the other. He delivers two addresses, with a brief sitting between them. He does not use strange language, and does not drawl, and is not indistinct.[195] The address should be brief, elegant, and comprehensive. It is liked that he recite a verse in the second also. Whoever enters while the speaker is making the address should not give the salutation. But if he gives a salutation, he has no right to have it returned, but a gesture in return is excellent. Also, he does not say, "Allah bless you," to those who sneeze.

These are the Stipulations for validity.

As for the Stipulations regarding the obligation to perform this Worship, it may be said, "The Friday Observance is not obligatory except upon the male who is mature, sane, Muslim, free, resident in a village that includes forty possession these qualities or in a village which is a suburb which is reached by the Call from the town on the side near it when the sounds have ceased and the *mu'adhdhin* has a high voice in accordance with the saying of Allah, When there is a call to the Worship on Friday hasten to the remembrance of Allah, and cease selling" (Qur'an, lxxii. 9). It is permitted to those to omit the Friday Observance on the excuse of rain, mud, fright, illness and attending to the sick when the sick one has no other attendant. Then it is desirable for them, I mean those who have excuses, to delay the Noon Worship until the people finish the Friday Observance. If there should be present at the Friday Observance one who is ill, or one on a journey, or a slave, or a woman, their Friday Observance is valid, and it serves as a substitute for the Noon Worship. And Allah knows better.

Exposition of the Proprieties of the Friday Observance, in Accordance with the Usual Order, including Ten Particulars

The first is that he prepares for the Friday Observance on Thursday, resolving upon performing it and anticipating its excellence. So he engages in Supplication and Seeking Forgiveness and in saying the Praise after *'asr,* mid-afternoon, on Thursday,

195. The other texts have "does not chant".

for the time of it, i.e. the hour after *'asr*, is equivalent[196] in excellence to "the hour" of Friday-Some one of the Fathers said, "Allah has a favour apart from the apportioned sustenance of mankind: none is given of that favour except one who asks for it on Thursday afternoon and on Friday."

He washes his clothes on that day and whitens them, prepares perfumes, if he has none, and empties his heart of the preoccupations which hinder it from early attendance at the Friday Observance. He states the intention, on this night, of fasting on Friday, for that has excellence. Let the fasting be connected with Thursday or Saturday, not be by itself, is for that is disliked. He engages in enlivening[197] this night by the performance of Worship and the complete recital of the Qur'an, for it has great excellence, and the excellence of Friday is drawn to it....Some relate the saying of Muhammad, "Allah is merciful to one who hastens and goes to the mosque early and causes his family to bathe and bathes himself." It is said, "Its meaning is, 'He washed his clothes,' for the word is handed down as *ghasala*, washed, [the other form was *ghassala*, caused to wash].

With this the proprieties of the anticipation of Friday are made complete, and he separates himself from the party of the unmindful, who, when they get up, say, "What is this day?" One of the Fathers said, "The man with the most perfect portion of the Friday Observance is the one who awaits it and observes it from the previous day. The one with the least portion is the one who says, when he gets up on Friday morning, 'What's to-day?'" One of them used to spend the night before Friday in the mosque on its account.

Second. When he rises be begins with bathing after the appearance of dawn. If he does not go out in the early morning,

---

196. The other texts read: "It is an hour that is compared to the 'undefined' hour."

197. "To cause the night to live" is to perform in it acts of devotion, such as "the Worship, supplication and intercession" (Sayyid Murtada, I, 209, 210, 1, 3). or, "the Worship, invocations, praises, the formulae for requesting forgiveness, blessing upon the Prophet and the completion of the recital of the Qur'an" (Sayyid Murtada, III, 241 A).

the nearer his bathing is to his going out to the mosque, the more liked it is, in order that it may be more close in time to the cleanness necessary for the Observance, for bathing is one of the assuredly liked acts. Some of the learned have held it to be an obligation. Muhammad said, "The bathing of the Friday Observance is obligatory upon everyone who has attained puberty." There is the *mashhur,* "well-known," tradition, handed down by Nafi'[198] from Ibn 'Umar, "Let whoever comes to the Friday Observance bathe!"

Muhammad said, "Let whoever is present at the Friday Observance, whether man or woman, bathe!"

When two of the people of Medina reviled one another, they used to say, one to the other, "Indeed you are worse than the one who does not bathe on Friday!"

'Umar said to 'Uthman, when he entered while he [i.e. 'Umar] was delivering the Friday address, "Is this the hour?" so expressing disapproval of him for omitting to come early. He replied, "I did nothing more, after I heard the Call to Worship, than perform the ablution and come out." So he said, "And the ablution too, when you know that the Messenger of Allah used to command us to bathe!" The allowability of omitting the complete bathing is known by the ablution of 'Uthman, and by what is related to the effect that Muhammad said, "If anyone performs the ablution on Friday, good and well, and whoever bathes--bathing is more excellent!"

Let whoever bathes for the legal impurity pour water over his body a second time with the Intention of its being for the bathing of the Friday Observance. If he must be content with one bathing it will suffice him and he will secure the excellence if he states the Intention of them both, for the bathing of the Friday Observance will enter into and become part of the bathing of the legal impurity. One of the Companions came upon his son who had just bathed, so he asked him, "Is it for the Friday Observance?" He replied, "Rather for legal impurity." So he said, "Do a second bathing," and he related the tradition of the washing

---

198. Abu 'Abdallah Nafi' b. Hurmuz al-Madani, *mawld* of Ibn 'Umar, a most reliable traditionist (d. 116 or 120 A.H.).

of the Friday Observance as obligatory upon every person who has attained puberty. He gave him the command only because he had not stated the Intention of doing it as a Friday bathing. It was not strange that it should be said, "The purpose is uncleanness," seeing that it is attained without the statement of the Intention. However, this position is impugnable in the case of the ablution also seeing it was made in the law a means of access, and its excellence must be sought. Whoever bathes and then becomes ceremonially unclean, does the ablution without invalidating his bathing, but it is more liked to guard against that.

The third is adornment. This is liked on this day. It is in three respects: clothing, cleanliness, and perfuming with scent.

(*a*) The cleanliness is attained by the use of the tooth stick, shaving the hair, paring the nails, cutting the moustache, and the rest of what has preceded in the Book of he Purification.[199] Ibn Mas'ud has said, "Whoever pares his nails on Friday has Allah expel from him disease and introduce into him healing." If he has entered the bathing place on Thursday or Wednesday he has attained the object.

(*b*) Let him perfume himself on this day with the best scent he has, to overcome disagreeable odours by it, and extend by it the essence and the scent to the noses of his neighbours who are present. The most liked perfume for man is the kind whose odour is apparent and whose colour is indistinguishable, and the perfume for women, whose colour is apparent and whose odour is indistinguishable. That is related in the Records of the Fathers. Al-Shafi' said, "Whoever cleans his garment decreases his anxiety, and whoever chooses a good scent increases his sense."

(*c*) As for the clothing, the best liked is white garments, since the best liked to Allah are white ones. One should not wear that which has something striking in it, and the wearing of black is not *sunnah,* Usage, and does not have excellence. Rather a company disliked to look at it, for it is an innovation that has taken place after the Messenger of Allah. The *'imamah*, "turban," is liked on this day.

---

199. This is Book III of the First Quarter of the *Ihya'* (Sayyid Murtada V, 302 ff).

Wathilah b. al-Asqa'[200] related that the Messenger of Allah said, "Allah and His angels bless the wearers of the turban on Friday." However, if the heat distresses one, there is no harm in his removing it before the Worship and after it, but he should not remove it during the time of his hastening from his residence to the Friday Observance, nor at the time of the Worship, nor when the *imam* ascends the pulpit nor during the address.

The fourth is going early to the congregational mosque. It is liked that he set out for the mosque from a distance of two or three parasangs [of three miles]. Let him go early. The time of going early begins with the appearance of the dawn. The excellence of going early is great. It is fitting that during his hastening to the Friday Observance he should be humble, lowly, stating the Intention of the *i'tikaf,* "the Retreat into the mosque for religious occupation" until [the end of[201]] the Worship, purposing to lose no time in answering the call of Allah to him to the Friday Observance and to hasten to obtain His forgiveness and the pleasing of Him.

Muhammad said, "Whoever goes to the Friday Observance in the first hour, it is as if he offered a camel. Whoever goes in the second hour, it is as if he offered a head of cattle. Whoever goes in the third hour, it is as if he offered a ram. Whoever goes in the fourth hour, it is as if he offered a chicken. Whoever goes in the fifth hour, it is as if he gave an egg. Then when the *imam* comes out, the leaves are rolled up, and the pens are raised, and the angels meet at the pulpit to hear the Invocation. so, whoever comes after that comes only for the duty of the Worship, and has nothing at all of the excellence." The first hour is until the appearance of the sun. The second is until its rising above the horizon. The third is to its broadening out, when the feet are burned,[202] and the fourth and fifth are after the middle of the morning until it passes the meridian. The excellence of these two is small--and the time of the passing of the meridian is the Worship's right and has no excellence attached to it.

---

200. Wathilah b. al-Asqa' al-Laithi, Companion (d. 83 or 85 or 86 A.H.).
201. This is added by Sayyid Murtada.
202. By the heat of the sun.

Muhammad said, "Three things there are, that men, if they knew what was in them, would ride their camels[203]] for. They are the Call, the first row, and the very early arrival at the Friday Observance." Ahmad b. Hanbal said, "The most excellent of them is the early arrival at the Friday Observance."

In Tradition it is said, "When it is Friday the angels sit on the doors of the mosques with leaves in their hands and pens of gold, writing the first as the first, according to their orders." It appears in the Records that "The angels miss a creature when he delays after his time on Friday, and they ask one another about him, 'What has such a one done, and what is it that delays him after his usual time?' So they say, 'O Allah! If poverty delays him, make him rich! If illness delays him, make him well! If work engages him, free him for Thy Divine service! If amusement delays him, turn toward him, that he may turn with his heart to Thine obedience!'"

In the first century, early at dawn and after the dawn, on Friday, the roads were seen full of men walking with lanterns, pressing together in the roads to the congregational mosques as in the Feast days, until that practice disappeared. It is said that the first innovation that occurred in Islam was the abandonment of going early to the mosque. And how should the Muslims not be ashamed before the Jews and Christians, seeing that they go early to the synagogues and churches on Saturday and Sunday, and the pursuers of this life go early to the open spaces around the congregational mosque, sell and seek profits, and why do those seeking the next abode not get ahead of them?

It is said, "Men will be near, when they look upon the Face of Allah, in proportion to the earliness of their going to the Friday Observance."

Ibn Mas'ud entered the mosque early and saw three persons who had preceded him in earliness, and was grieved at that and began to say to himself, blaming himself, "The fourth of four!" And yet the fourth of four is early.

The fifth is the manner of entry. One should not pass over the necks of the people, nor pass before them, earliness making

203. The other text has "they would run like camels."

that easy for him, for a very great threat has been issued regarding stepping over the necks, which is that he is made a bridge on Resurrection Day that men will step over. Ibn Juraij[204] has related a *mursal*[205] tradition, "lacking the authority of a Companion," that the Messenger of Allah, while he was giving the Friday address, saw a man stepping over the necks of the people until he got in front, and then he sat down. So after the Prophet had finished his Worship he went towards the man until he caught up with him and said, "O such a one! what hindered you from celebrating the Friday Observance with us to-day?" He said, "Prophet of Allah! I have celebrated the Friday Observance with you." So the Prophet said, "Did I not see you stepping over the necks of the people?" He indicated by it that he had rendered his work useless.

In a *musnad*, "supported," tradition it is related that he said, "What hindered you from worshipping with us?" He replied, "And did you not see me?" So Muhammad said, "I saw you; you procrastinated, and you did harm!" That is, "you were late from the early attendance, and you harmed the attendance."

Whenever the first row is left empty one may step over the necks of the people, for they have lost their right and have left the place of excellence. Al-Hasan said, "Step over the necks of the people who sit upon the doorways of the mosques on Friday, for they do not deserve any respect."[206]

When there are not in the mosque any but those who are at the Worship, it is fitting that he should not give the greeting, for it imposes the responsibility of an answer that would be out of place.

The sixth is that one does not pass before the people. He sits by himself, near a column or a wall, so that they may not pass before him, I mean, before the worshipper, for, although that does not stop the Worship, it is something prohibited. Muhammad said, "Indeed, that he should stand forty years were better for him than

---

204. 'Abd al-Malik b. 'Abd al-'Aziz b. Juraij al-Makki, *mawla* Bani Umayyah (d. 149-51, 155 A.H.).

205. Sayyid Murtada states that it lacks also the Successor's authority, and therefore is what is technically called *mu'dal*.

206. Strictly, "they have no individuality".

to pass before a worshipper."

Muhammad said, "Indeed, that a man should be ashes, fine and copious, which the winds blow away, were better for him than that he should pass before one who is worshipping."

It has been related in another tradition, regarding the passer and the worshipper, when the latter worships in the road and comes short in repelling the passer, that Muhammad said, "If the one passing in front of a worshipper and the worshipper himself could know their responsibility in that regard they would know that to stand forty years would be better for him than to pass before him."

The column and the wall and the worship-mat as spread out are a bound for the worshipper, so he should repel whoever passes by it.

Muhammad said, "Let him repel him, and, if he objects [still let him repel him, and, if he objects[207]] let him contend with him, for he is a devil."

Abu Sa'id al-Khudri[208] used to repel whoever passed before him to the extent that he threw him down, for perhaps the men hung on to him. Then the man implored the protection of Mirwan[209] against him, and then he would inform him that the Prophet ordered him to do that.

If any should not find a column let him set up before him something about a cubit long, in order that that may be an indication of his boundary.

The seventh is that he seeks the first row, for its excellence is great, as we have related in the tradition. In Tradition it is related, "Whoever causes his family to bath and bathes himself and hastens and arrives early at the mosque and gets near the *imam* and hearkens, has that as an atonement for what he committed between the two Friday Observances, along with three days extra." And in another version, it says, "Allah forgives him

---

207. Sayyid Murtada omits this repetition.
208. Abu Sa'id Sa'd b. Malik al-Khudri al-Ansari (d. 74 A.H.).
209. Mirwan b. al-Hakim b. Abu al-'As al-Umawi (d. 65 A.H.), fourth Umayyad khalifah.

until the next Friday Observance." It is stipulated in one of the versions that he should not step over the necks of the people.

In seeking the first row, one should not be unmindful of three things: (a) The first of them is that, when he is used to seeing, near the one giving the address, a thing disapproved by Allah, which he is unable to change, such as the wearing of silk on the part of the *imam* or someone else, or worship with a heavy weapon, which engages the attention, or a golden weapon, or something else which ought to be disapproved, then to be in back is more safe, and more concentrating for careful thought. So did a company of the learned, seeking safety.

It was said to Bishr b. al-Harith,[210] "We notice that you go early but worship in the last of the rows." So he said, "Nearness of hearts only is desired, not nearness of bodies." He indicated by it that the rear gave him greater safety of heart. Sufyan al-Thawri looked at Shu'aib b. Harb[211] near the pulpit, listening to an address from Abu Ja'far al-Mansur.[212] So after he finished the Worship he said, "Your nearness to this man disturbed my heart. Were you safe in hearing a speech, the disapproval of which is incumbent upon you, and you do not do so?" Then Sufyan mentioned what the tradition said about wearing black. So he replied, "O Abu 'Abdallah! is it not related in Tradition, 'Draw near and hear?' Then he answered, 'Woe to you! That refers to the khalifahs,[213] the orthodox, the rightly-guided, but as for these, the more you keep your distance from them and do not consider them, the nearer you are to Allah!"

Sa'id b. 'Amir[214] said, "I performed a Worship at the side of Abu al-Darda', and then he began to go back in the rows until

---

210. Abu Muhammad Bishr b. Mansur al-Sulami (d. 209 A.H.).
211. Shu'aib b. Harb (Abu Salih) al-Mada'ini (d. 197 A.H.).
212. Abu Ja'far al-Mansur (d. 158), second Abbasid khalifah.
213. Sayyid Murtada says these are the first four and also 'Umar b. 'Abd al'Aziz.
214. Sa'id b. 'Amir, Successor, unknown; Ibn Khalfun was sure he was Sa'id b. 'Amir b. Khudhaim (Judhaim in Sayyid Murtada is a misprint), but Ibn Hajar objected that the latter died in the khalifate of 'Umar I. Bin Khudhaim, according to the *Tajrid Asma' al-Sahabah*, governed Hims for 'Umar I (p. 240).

we were in the last row. So after we had done the Worship I said to him, 'Is it not said, "The best of the rows is the first of them?"' He replied, 'Yes, only, this people is one that has obtained mercy, and is given regard from among the peoples, and Allah, when He gives regard to a people in the Worship, forgives him and whoever of mankind is behind him. So I went back only hoping that He would forgive me on account of one whom Allah regards.' "

One of the traditionists relates that he said, "I heard the Messenger of Allah say that." So, whoever stays back for this purpose, preferring and manifesting excellence of disposition, does no harm, and of this it is said, "Works are to be judged by intentions."

(b) The second is that, if there is no enclosure[215] near the one giving the address, separated from the mosque for the use of the sultans, then the first row is liked. (Otherwise the enclosure is to be preferred.[216]) But some of the learned have expressed dislike of entering the enclosure. Al-Hasan and Bakr al-Muzani were wont not to worship in the enclosure, considering that it was restricted to the use of the sultans, as it is an innovation in the mosques that occurred after the time of the Messenger of Allah. A mosque is free for all men, and that enclosure was cut off in contradiction to this principle.

Anas b. Malik and 'Imran b. Hasin worshipped in the enclosure, and did not express dislike of that, out of desire for nearness. Perhaps the dislike is especially for its exclusiveness and the prohibition (against others worshipping in it[217]), but as for the single matter of the enclosure, if there is no prohibition, dislike of it is not obligatory.

(c) The third is that the pulpit cuts some of the rows. The first row is only the one continuous row which is in the space in the front of the pulpit, and what is on its two sides is cut off. Al-Thawri used to say, "The first row is the outside one in front

215. Sayyid Murtada adds that these were first built in the times of al-Umayyah out of fear of enemies.
216. This is omitted by Sayyid Murtada.
217. This is added by Sayyid Murtada.

of the pulpit," and it is reasonable, because it is continuous and because the one sitting in it faces the one giving the address and hears him. It might be said, "The one nearest to the *qiblah* is the first row, and no regard is paid here to (the pulpit)."[218]

Worship in the bazars and the open spaces outside the mosque is disliked. Some of the Companions used to beat the men and make them get up from the open spaces.

The eighth is that one cuts off one's preliminary Worship when the *imam* comes out (to ascend the pulpit[219]), and he stops talking also. Rather, he occupies himself with the reply to the *mu'adhdhin,* and then with hearing the address. It was the custom of some of the common people to make a Prostration at the standing up of the *mu'adhdhins* (for the Call to Worship), but there is no basis established for it in any record or tradition. But if it fits in with a Prostration of Recital there is no harm in it, for it is an excellent time to make a supplication, and there is no judgment of unlawfulness against this Prostration, for there is no cause to make it unlawful. It is related from 'Ali and 'Uthman that they said, "Whoever listens and is silent has two rewards; whoever does not listen and is silent has one rewards; whoever hears and lets a word[220] slip has two sins against him, and whoever does not bear and lets a word slip has one."

Muhammad said, "Whoever says to his companion, while the *imam* is making the address, 'Be silent,' or 'Hush', has himself let a word slip, and whoever lets a word slip while the *imam* is making the address has no Friday Observance to his credit." This indicates that causing others to be silent should be by gesture, or by throwing a pebble, not by utterance.

In the tradition of Abu Dharr[221] it is stated, "When he questioned Ubayy while the Prophet was making an address and said, 'When was this *surah* sent down?' Ubayy gestured to him to keep silent. So when the Messenger of Allah came down from the pulpit Ubayy said to him, 'Go, and you have no Friday

---

218. The other texts read "to this meaning".
219. This is Sayyid Murtada's explanation.
220. This is Sayyid Murtad'a's definition.
221. Abu Dharr al-Ghifari, Companion (d. 32 or 33 A.H.).

Observance.' So Abu Dharr complained to the Prophet, and he relied, 'Ubayy spoke the truth.'"

If anyone is far from the *imam* it is not fitting that he should talk, about learning or anything else, but rather keep silent, since all that has its chain of consequences, and results in murmuring, so that it reaches the listeners. He does not sit in a circle with anyone who is speaking. So, let whoever is unable to listen on account of his distance keep quiet, for that is liked. Since the Worship is disliked in the time of the address of the *imam,* much more is talking disliked. 'Ali said, "The Worship is disliked at four times: after *'asr*, 'mid-afternoon', at mid-day and while the *imam* is making the address."

The ninth is that he observe, in following out the *imam's* pattern in the Friday Observance, that which we have mentioned in regard to the other Worships. So, when he hears the Recital of the *imam,* he does not recite anything but the Fatihah, When he finishes the Friday Observance he recites the *surah* of "The Praise[222] belongs to Allah" (i), and, "Say, It (the fact) is, Allah is One!" (cxii), and the two *surahs* of Seeking Refuge (cxiii., cxiv.), each seven times. One of the Fathers related that whoever does that is preserved from sin from one Friday Observance to the next Friday Observance, for it is a guard for him against Satan.

It is liked that he say, after the Friday Observance, "O Allah! O Rich One! O One of Praise! O Beginner! O Returner! O Merciful! O Loving One! make me, by Thy lawful things, do without Thine unlawful things, and, by Thy favour, any other besides Thyself!" It is said, "Whoever perseveres in this supplication has Allah make him do without His creatures, 'and apportions him a sustenance from a source he does not expect'" (Qur'an, lxv. 2).

Then, after the Friday Observance, he performs a Worship of six *rak'ahs*. Ibn 'Umar has related that Muhammad used, after the Friday Observance, to perform a Worship of two *rak'ahs,* and Abu Hurairah states four, and 'Ali and 'Abdallah b. 'Abbas six and all are valid, in different circumstances, and the most complete is the Friday most excellent.

---

222. This is one of the names of the Fatihah; the list of them is given in Sayyid Murtada, V, 132 C.

The tenth is that he remains at the congregational mosque until he performs the *'asr* Worship, and if he should remain until the Sunset one, that would be most excellent. It is said, "Whoever performs the *'asr*, 'mid-afternoon,' Worship in the mosque has the reward of a Pilgrimage, and whoever performs the Sunset one has the reward of a Pilgrimage and a minor visit to the Ka'bah."

If he is not safe against merely affecting a goodly way and against the coming of evil (e.g., pride) upon him from men's looking upon him in his Worship in retreat, or, if he fears wading into something that does not concern him, it is more excellent that he should return to his house, invoking the remembrance of Allah, considering His benefits, thanking Allah for His giving of help, fearful of his coming short, watching over his heart and his tongue until the setting of the sun, so that the "hour of honour" may not escape him. He does not engage, in the congregational mosque or the other mosques, in talk of this life. Muhammad said, "There will come upon men a time when their talk in the mosques will be of this life's concern. Allah is not in need of them, so do not sit with them."

Exposition of the Proprieties and Usages Not Included in the Preceding Arrangements

This applies to the whole day and is in seven particulars.

The first is that he is present at the assemblies of learning in the early morning and after mid-afternoon, and does not attend the gatherings of the story-tellers, for there is no benefit in their talk. It is fitting that the devotee should not be unoccupied during the whole of Friday with good deeds and supplications, so that the "hour of honour" may meet him while he is at some good. It is not fitting that he should be present at the circles of men before the Worship. 'Abdallah b. 'Umar related that the Prophet forbade sitting in a circle on Friday before the Worship, unless there is one knowing about Allah, who reminds of the days of Allah, and gives understanding in the religion of Allah, speaking in the congregational mosque in the early morning. Then he may sit before him and so will be uniting early attendance and hearing. The hearing of learning beneficial in the next abode is more excellent than his occupying himself with supererogatory performances of the Worship. For Abu Dharr has related that presence at an assembly of learning is more excellent than a Worship of a thousand *rak'ahs.*

Anas b. Malik said, about the saying of Allah, "And when the Worship is finished, scatter abroad in the earth, and desire some of the favours of Allah" (Qur'an, lxii. 10), "Is it not that it is not seeking this life, but visiting some sick one, and being present at a funeral, and acquiring learning and calling on a brother in Allah?" Allah has called learning excellent in a number of places. He said, "And He taught you what you did not know, and the favour of Allah to you was great" (Qur'an, iv. 113). He said, "And We indeed brought David favour" (Qur'an, xxxiv. 10), meaning learning. So acquire learning on this day. Teaching is one of the most excellent of good works. Worship is more excellent than sitting with the story-tellers, since they were used to consider it an innovation, and to exclude story-tellers from the congregational mosque.

Ibn 'Umar was present[223] at his place of sitting in the congregational mosque, and behold, a story-teller was telling a story in his place. So he said, "Get up from my sitting place!" Then he replied, "I'll not get up, for I have sat down and got to it before you!" So Ibn 'Umar went to the master of the guard and he got him up. But if that (i.e., story-telling) were a part of the *sunnah,* Usage, to get him up would not have been lawful, for, indeed, Muhammad has said, "Do not, by any means, any of you, get his brother up from his sitting-place and then sit there, but make room and be comfortable." Ibn 'Umar, whenever a man got up for him from his sitting-place, used not to sit in it until the man should return to it. It is related that a story-teller sat in the space before the room of 'A'ishah, so she sent to Ibn 'Umar, "This one has harmed me by his stories, and distracted me from my Supererogatory Worship." So Ibn 'Umar beat him until he broke his stick over him, and then cast him out.

The second is that he watch well for the "hour of honour", for, in the *mashhur,* "well-known," tradition, it is related that on Friday there is an hour that no Muslim creature meets while asking something of Allah without His giving it to him. In another

---

223. The other texts read "went early to".

tradition it is said, "Does not come upon it while worshipping." There is disagreement for it is said, "It is the hour of the appearing of the sun," and it is said, "It is the passing of the meridian," and it is said, "with the Call to Worship," and it is said, "When the *imam* mounts the pulpit and begins the address," and it is said, "When the people stand up for the Worship," and it is said, "The last part of the time of *'asr*, 'mid-afternoon,' I mean, in the 'hour of preference,' "[224] and it is said, "Before the setting of the sun."[225] Fatimah[226] used to observe that time, and order her servant to look at the sun, and inform her of its going down. Then she would begin with Supplication and Seeking Forgiveness, until the sun set, and she used to relate that hour was the one waited for, and that she handed it on from her father. Some of the learned said, "It is undefined during the whole day, like the Night of Decree, so that those who supplicate may do much watching for it." It is said, "It moves about among the hours of Friday, like the moving about of the Night of Decree." And this is the more likely. It has a mystery which it is not fitting to mention in the Science of Practical Religion. Notwithstanding, it is fitting that he should believe that Muhammad said, "Your Lord has in the days of your age gifts. Is it not so? Therefore, address yourselves to them."

Friday is one of that whole number of days, so it is fitting that the creature should be, during the whole day, attentive to

---

224. The 'asr is divided by al-Bajuri into five periods, as regards the acceptability of the Worship, termed the times of (1) excellence; (2) preference; (3) allowability; (4) allowable but disliked; and (5) prohibition. Others add (6) the time of necessity, which is the last when it may be done; (7) excusable, at noon; (8) the time of overtaking; and finally (9) the time when the Substitution payment is made.

    The sunset has one period; the evening has two, of preference and of allowability; the morning has five, and noon has one extended period. Al-Bajuri, *Commentary on Abu Shuja'*, I, 128f.; *Kitab al-Salah, fasl* i.

225. Sayyid Murtada says there are more than twenty statements about it, and al-Ghazzali mentions only as many as Abu Talib has in the *Qut al-Qulub*.

226. Fatimah, the daughter of Muhammad (d. 11 A.H.).

it, by presenting his heart and continuing in the remembering, and discarding the evil suggestions of this life. Then perhaps he will have the good fortune to obtain some of those gifts. Ka'b al-Ahbar has said, "It is in the last hour of Friday, and that is at the setting of the sun." Then Abu Hurairah said, "And how is it the last hour, when I heard the Messenger of Allah say, 'No creature who is worshipping meets it,' but the setting of the sun is not a time for Worship?" Then Ka'b replied, "Did not the Messenger of Allah say, "Whoever sits down waiting for the Worship is himself at Worship'?" He replied, "Yes, indeed!" He rejoined, "So then, that is Worship!" And Abu Hurairah kept silent. Ka'b was inclined to the idea that it was a mercy of Allah to those who performed the rightful duties of this day, and the time of sending it was at the finishing of the work.

In short, this time is honourable, along with the time of the *imam*'s mounting of the pulpit, so let him increase supplication at those two times.

The third is that it is liked to increase the intercession for the Messenger of Allah on this day. For Muhammad said, "Whoever performs the intercession, *salah,* for me on Friday eighty times, has Allah forgive him the sins of eighty years."

It was said, "Messenger of Allah, what is the manner of the intercession for you?" He replied, "You say, 'O Allah, bless (*salli'ala*), Muhammad, Thy creature, Thy Prophet, Thy Messenger, the unlettered[227] Prophet,' and count one. It is also well if you should say, 'O Allah, bless Muhammad and the family of Muhammad with a blessing, *salah* that to Thee is pleasing and of his right is a fulfilment, and give him access and send him to the station of glory that Thou didst promise him, and reward him on our behalf what he is worth, and reward him on our behalf the most excellent of that with which Thou hast rewarded any prophet on behalf of his people, and bless him and all his brethren among the prophets and among the righteous, O Thou most merciful of those showing Mercy.'" You say this seven times, for

227. *Al-ummi,* says Sayyid Murtada, may mean "unlettered," or "Meccan," or "the one with the Fatihah, the Mother of the Book" (Sayyid Murtada, II, 34 D).

it has been said "Whoever says it on seven Fridays seven times each Friday has obligatory for him the intercession of Muhammad."

If one wishes to do more, let him bring the traditional intercession (*salah*) and say, "O Allah, cause the excellence of Thy blessing, Thy growing benefactions and the honour of Thy benevolences, mercy and felicitation to come upon Muhammad, who is the chief of those sent by Thee, the leader of those fearing Thee, the Seal of the Prophets, the Messenger of the Lord of the worlds, the Captain of Good and the Conqueror of Righteousness, the Prophet of Mercy and the Chief of the People. O Allah, send him to a station of glory through which his nearness increases and by which his eye is refreshed and on account of which the first and the last emulate him without envy. O Allah, give him favour, excellence, honour, access, the exalted degree and the lofty, overtopping position. O Allah, give Muhammad his request, extend him his hope, make him the first intercessor, and the first successful intercessor. O Allah, establish his argument, weigh down his balance, make effective his cause, and exalt his degree among the highest of those with Thee. O Allah, assemble us in the party and make us to be of the people of his intercession! Make us live according to his Usage, and cause us to die according to his religious party, and bring us to his watering place, and give us drink in his cup, unashamed, not regretting, not doubting, not changing, not trying others, and not tried! *Amin*! O Lord of the Worlds!"

In short, whatever expression of the blessing one uses, even though it should be the well-known expression of the Witnessing, he is one that is saying the Blessing upon the Prophet. It is fitting that he should join to it the Seeking Forgiveness, for that also is liked on this day.

The fourth is the Recital of the Qur'an. So let him recite much of it. Let him recite the Surat al-Khaf, Cave (xviii.), especially, for it has been related from Ibn 'Abbas and Abu Hurairah in a tradition traced back to the Prophet that whoever recites the Surat al-Kahf on the eve of Friday or on Friday is given a light from where he recites it to Mecca, and he is forgiven until the next Friday, along with three days extra, and 70,000 angels intercede for him until he enters upon the morning and he is preserved from illness, disease of the stomach, pleurisy, leprosy, elephantiasis and the testing of the Antichrist.

It is liked that he finish a recital of the Qur'an on Friday and the eve of Friday, if he can, and let his finishing be in the two *rak'ahs* of the Dawn Worship if he has been reciting in the night, or in the two *rak'ahs* of the Sunset Worship, or between the Call to Worship and the Institution of the Friday Observance, for it has great excellence. The pious, *'abidun,* used to like to recite on Friday, "Say, He is Allah, One!" (cxii.) a thousand times. It is said, "Whoever recites it in ten *rak'ahs,* or twenty, does what is more excellent than an entire recital of the Qur'an."

They used to make intercession for the Prophet a thousand times. They used to say, "O the Praise of Allah," and "The Praise is Allah's" and "There is no god but Allah," and "Allah is greater," a thousand times. If he recites the six Praises on Friday or the eve of Friday it is well. It is not recorded from the Prophet that he used to recite the *surahs* in their total substance except on Friday, and on the eve of Friday.

He used to recite at the Sunset Worship of the eve of Friday, "Say, O ye unbelievers!" (cix.) and "Say, He is Allah, One!" (cxii.). He used to recite in the last of the evening Worships on the eve of Friday, Surat al-Jumu'ah (lxii.) and al-Munafiqun (lxiii.). It is related that he used to recite them both in the two *rak'ahs* of the Friday Observance. He used to recite in the Morning Worship of Friday Surah Sajdat Luqman (xxxi.), and Surat al-Dahr (lxxvi.), "Has there come upon men?"

The fifth is the performances of the Worship. It is liked, when one enters the congregational mosque, not to sit down until he performs four *rak'ahs* in which he recites, "Say, He is Allah, One" (cxii.) two hundred times, in each *rak'ah* fifty times. For it is handed down from the Messenger of Allah that whoever does so will not die until he sees his place of sitting in the Garden, or it is seen for him.

He should not omit the two *rak'ahs* of the Greeting, even if the *imam* should be making the address, but he should be brief. The Messenger of Allah ordered that. In a *gharib,*[228] "strange,"

---

228. *Gharib,* "strange" "rare"; if a tradition is transmitted by only one definite person of later generations, it is called *gharib* in reference to that person.

tradition, it is related that Muhammad kept silent for one entering the mosque until he performed the two *rak'ahs*. The Kufis said, "If the *imam* pauses for him, he performs them."

It is liked on this day that he should perform a Worship of four *rak'ahs* with the four *surahs* of al-An'am (vi.), al-Kahf (xviii.), Ta-Ha (xx.), and Ya-Sin (xxxvi.). If he cannot recite them well he recites Surah Ya-Sin, Surah Sajdah Luqman (xxxi.), Surat al-Dukhan (xliv.) and Surat al-Mulk (lxvii.). He should not omit reciting the four *surahs* on the eve of Friday, for there is great excellence in them. Whoever cannot recite them well should then recite what he can do well, and it is equal to the complete recital of the Qur'an for him. He should do much of the recital of the Surat al-Ikhlas (cxii).

It is liked that he should perform the Worship of the Praise, according to the manner that shall be mentioned in the Chapter on the Voluntary Worship, for Muhammad said to his uncle, 'Abbas,[229] "Use it in the Worship on every Friday." Ibn 'Abbas was wont not to omit performing this act of Worship on Friday after the passing of the meridian, and used to tell of the grandeur of its excellence. The best is that he should devote his time up to the passing of the meridian to the Worship itself, and after the Friday Observance until mid-afternoon, to the hearing of learning, and after that until sunset, to the Praise, and the Asking of Forgiveness.

The sixth is almsgiving. It is liked on this day and excels in excellence on this day especially, for it is multiplied, except for one who asks while the *imam* is making the address, and talks during the address of the *imam*, for this is disliked. Salih b. Muhammad[230] said, "A poor man begged on Friday at the side of my father. So a man gave a bit to hand it to him, but my father did not take it from him." Ibn Mas'ud said, "Whenever a man begs in the mosque he is worthy not to receive. Whenever he begs on the Qur'an, do not give to him." Of the learned there

229. Abu al-Fadl 'Abbas b. 'Abd al-Muttalib, uncle of Muhammad (d. 32 A.H.).
230. Salih b. Ahmad b. Muhammad b. Hanbal al-Shaibani (d. 265, 266 A.H.).

are some who dislike giving alms to beggars in the congregational mosques, who step over the necks of the people, unless he beg standing or sitting in his place without stepping over.

Ka'b al-Ahbar said, "Whoever is present at the Friday Observance and then goes out and gives two different things of the things that are given as alms, and then returns and performs two *rak'ahs,* completing their Bowing, their Prostration and their humbleness, and then says, 'O Allah, I ask Thee by Thy name, in the name of Allah, the Merciful and Compassionate, in the name of Him besides Whom there is no God, the Living, the Self-Existent, whom neither slumber takes nor sleep,' does not ask Allah anything but He gives it."

Some one of the Fathers said, "Whoever feeds a poor man on Friday and then goes early and is early at the congregational mosque, and does not harm anyone, and then, when the *imam* gives the Salutation at the close of the Worship, says, 'In the name of Allah, the Merciful and Compassionate, the Living, the Self-Existent One, I ask Thee that Thou forgive me and have mercy on me, and preserve me from the Fire,' and then makes supplication for what seems good to him, is answered."

The seventh is that he should spend Friday for the next abode. So he withdraws in its from all the works of this life, and does many *wirds,*[231] "devotional recitals," in it. He should not begin a journey in it, for it is related that whoever makes a journey on the eve and early part of Friday has his two angels invoke curses upon him, for it is forbidden after the appearance of dawn, except when the company of fellow travellers will pass on. Some of the Fathers disliked buying water in the mosque from the water-carrier, for drinking or donating it, in order that it might not be bought in the mosque, for selling and buying in the mosque are disliked. But they said, "There is no harm, were he to give the bit of money outside the mosque, and then drink it or donate it to others as a religious service in the mosque."

In short, he should, on Friday, do more of his *wirds*, Recitals, and of his various good works, for whenever Allah loves a creature, He occupies him in the excellent times in excellent works.

---

231. This is Book X of the first Quarter of the *Ihya'*.

Whenever He hates him, He occupies him in the excellent times in evil deeds, that may be more productive of pain in his punishment and more intensifying of the hate of him, because of his refusal of the blessing of the time and his violation of the sacredness of the time.

On Friday, certain *du'a's,* Supplications, are liked, and mention of them will be made in the Book of *Da'awat,*[232] Supplications, if Allah will, and may Allah bless every elect creature!

---

232. This is Book IX of the first Quarter of the *Ihya'.*

6

Various Problems Which Cause General Distress and Which the Devotee Needs to Know

The problems which are of rare occurrence we have investigated in the Books of *Fiqh,* Canon Law.

The Problem of the Slight Act. Although it does not invalidate the Worship, it is disliked, unless there is need for it. That kind of act is the repelling of a passers-by and the killing of a scorpion that one fears and can kill with one or two blows, but whenever they become three, they are too many, and invalidate the Worship. Similarly, one may get rid of a louse and a flea, whenever one suffers from them. Similarly, his need of scratching, which disturbs him from humbleness. Ma'adh used to catch a louse and a flea, during the Worship, and Ibn 'Umar used to kill a louse and a flea during the Worship, so that the blood would appear on his hand. Al-Nakha'i said, "You catch it and disable it and there is nothing against one if one kill it." Ibn Musayyab said, "He takes it and benumbs it and then throws it down." Mujahid[233] said, "The most liked thing, in my opinion, is to let it alone, unless it causes one suffering, and so distracts one from one's Worship, and then one should disable it enough so that it will not cause one suffering and then throw it away."

This is a permission only, and otherwise the perfect thing is to guard against the action, even if it be slight. On that account one of them was accustomed not to brush away a fly, for he said, "I will not accustom myself to it, so that it may corrupt my Worship

---

233. He is not further defined, but is probably Abu Hajjah Muhahid b. Jahr (Jubair, in Ibn Khallikan), Successor (d. 101-103 or 111 A.H.

for me, seeing that I have heard that criminals before kings are patient under great suffering, and do not move."

Whenever a person yawns, there is no harm in putting his hand over his mouth, which is preferable. If he sneezes he says, "O the Praise of Allah!" to himself, and does not move his tongue. If he belches, he should not raise his head to the sky. If his cloak falls, he should not rearrange it, and so with the ends of his turban, for that is disliked, unless it is necessary.

The Problem of Worship in Sandals. It is permissible, *ja'iz*, even though removing the sandals is easy. The permission with regard to the leather socks is not on account of the difficulty of removing them, but, rather, this uncleanness is pardonable. Footwear in general comes under the meaning of leather socks. The Messenger of Allah performed worship in his sandals. Then he removed them, so the people removed their sandals. Then he said, "Why did you remove your sandals?" They replied, "We saw you remove yours, so we removed ours." He said, "Gabriel came to me to tell me that they had some dirt on them, so whenever any one of you sets out for the mosque, let him turn up his sandals, and let him look at them, and if he sees any dirt, let him scrape them on the ground, and let him worship in them."

One of them said, "Worship in sandals is more excellent because Muhammad said, 'Why did you remove your sandals?'" This is going too far, for he questioned them to show them the reason for his removing his sandals, since he knew that they removed theirs to be in accord with him.

'Abdallah b. al-Sa'ib[234] has related that the Prophet removed his sandals. So then, he did both things. But it is not fitting that one who removes his should put them on his right or his left, for that restricts the space, and cuts off the row. Rather he puts them in front of him, and does not leave them behind him, for his heart would be turning to them. Perhaps the one who thinks that Worship in them is more excellent has this idea, that is, the turning of the heart of them.

Abu Hurairah related that the Prophet said, "Whenever one of you performs a Worship, let him put his sandals between his

234. 'Abdallah b. Sa'ib, Companion, Meccan reciter of the Qur'an.

feet." Abu Hurairah said to someone else, "Place them between your feet and do not trouble any Muslim by them." The Messenger of Allah placed them at his left, while he was acting as *imam.* So the *imam* may do that, since no one stands at his left. It is preferable that he should not put them between his feet, for they would engage his attention, but before his feet. Perhaps that is the meaning of the tradition. Jubair b. Mut'im[235] said, "A man's placing his sandals between his feet is an innovation."

A Problem. Whenever he expectorates in his Worship, his Worship is not invalidated, because it is a minor act. Whatever sound does not result from is not reckoned as speech, and is not of the form of the letters of speech, only it is disliked. So, one must guard against it, except that the Messenger of Allah gave permission about it, since one of the Companions related that the Messenger of Allah saw in the *qiblah* direction an expectoration mark, and then became very angry. "Then he scrapped it with a palm-branch that was in his hand, and said, 'Bring me some mixed perfume.' So he smeared over the mark with saffron. Then he turned to us and said, 'What one of you likes to be spit on in the face?' We said, 'Not one of us.' He replied, 'Then any one of you, whenever he enters upon the Worship, has Allah between himself and the *qiblah,*' and, in another version, 'has Allah facing him'. So let not any one of you expectorate in front of his face, nor on his right, but to his left, or beneath his left foot, but if it should unexpectedly proceed from him, let him spit into his garment, and let him make it slight, and rub one part with another."

Another Problem. The standing of the imitator of the *imam* has *sunnah,* Usage, and *fard,* Prescribed, aspects. The Usage is that he stands at the right of the *imam,* drawn back from him a little. A woman alone should stand behind the *imam,* although if she should stand beside the *imam,* that would not be harmful, but she would contravert the Usage. If there should be a man with her, the man should stand at the right of the *imam,* and she behind the man. He should not stand behind the row by himself, but rather enter into the row himself, or draw to himself one from

---

235. Jubair b. Mut'im Companion (d. 57-59 A.H.).

the row. But if he should stand by himself, his Worship would be valid, along with dislike.

The *fard*, Prescribed, part is the continuity of the row, i.e., that there should be between the imitator and the *imam* a connecting bond, since they are in a company. So if they are in a mosque, that is sufficient as a connection, for it was built for that, and there is no need for continuity of row, but rather for this that he be cognizant of the actions of the *imam*.

Abu Hurairah performed a Worship of an *imam* on the roof of a mosque. Whenever the follower is in the front of the mosque, in the roadway, or the open space adjoining, and there is no obstacle of masonry separating them, the nearness of the measure of the distance of the bowshot of an arrow is sufficient. There is sufficient bond in the Worship when the action of one of them reaches the other. But continuation is stipulated only when one stands in the courtyard of a house at the right of the mosque, or the left, with its door cleaving to the mosque, and the Stipulation is that the row of the mosque extend in the courtyard's passageway, without a break, to the court. Then the Worship of whoever is in that row and behind is valid, but not the Worship of the one who is in front of it. This is the rule of the separated buildings, but a single building and a single court are like an open space.

Another Problem. (a) Whenever the late-comer arrives in time for the last of the Worship of the *imam*, that is the first of his Worship. So let him come into accord with the *imam*, and let him build upon that, and let him recite the *qunut*, Supplication, in the morning at the last of his own Worship, even though he has recited the *qunut*, Supplication, in the morning at the last of his own Worship, even though he has recited the *qunut*, Supplication, along with the *imam*.

(b) If he is in time for part of the Standing Posture along with the *imam*, he should not engage in the Supplications, but let him begin with the Fatihah, and let him do it quickly. Then, if the *imam* does the Bowing before he finishes the Fatihah, and he is able to catch up with him on his rising from the Bowing, let him finish it. But if he is unable, he gets into accord with the *imam* and bows when he does. A part of the Fatihah has the authority of the whole of it, so the Fatihah falls away from him because of their going ahead of him. If the *imam* bows while he is in the midst of reciting the *surah*, let him break it off.

(c) If he overtakes the *imam* in the Sitting or the Witnessing portions of the Worship, he says the *takbirat al-ihram*, and then he sits. He does not say the *takbir* of the transitions when he overtakes the *imam* in the Bowing, for he says the *takbir*, a second time in the bending over, for that is a transition reckoned to belong to it, and the *takbirs* are for the original transitions in the Worship, not for incidents on account of the imitation of the *imam* on the part of the follower who is late. But he does not overtake the *rak'ah* so long as he does not come to rest in bowing while the *imam* is still within the time limit of those bowing with him. For, if his coming to rest at the Bowing is not complete until after the *imam* has passed out of the time limit of those bowing, that *rak'ah* escapes him.

A Problem. (a) Let anyone whom the Noon Worship escapes up to the time of mid-afternoon perform the Noon Worship first, and then the Afternoon one. But if he begins with the Afternoon Worship, that may do, but he has left what is preferable, and heedlessly risked the appearance of heterodoxy. However, if he finds an *imam* to follow, let him perform the Afternoon Worship and then let him perform the Noon Worship after it. The Congregational Worship has first claim to performance.

(b) But if he performs a Worship by himself in the early part of the period, and then overtakes the Congregational Worship, he should perform the Worship in the congregation, and state the Intention of the Worship of the time, and Allah will take account of whichever one He wills.

(c) But if he states the Intention of a Worship that escaped, or a *tatawwu*, Voluntary, Worship, it is permitted.

(d) If he has just performed a Worship in the congregation, and then overtakes another congregation, let him state the Intention of an escaped Worship, or a *nafl*, Supererogatory, Worship, for the repetition of the payment of the Worship in the congregation another time has no reason, and is admissible only for the sake of securing the excellence of the Congregational Worship.

Another Problem. When one has performed a Worship, and then sees on one's garment of some uncleanness, the most liked thing is to perform a Substitute Worship, but it is not incumbent upon one and if one should see the uncleanness is the midst of the Worship, one casts off the garment and finishes the Worship. The most liked is beginning again. The basis for this is the story of the Prophet's taking off his sandals when Gabriel informed the Messenger of Allah that there was some uncleanness upon them, for he did not begin the Worship anew.

Another Problem. Anyone who leaves out the First Witnessing or the *qunut*, Supplication, or leaves out the Blessing for the Messenger of Allah, in the First Witnessing, or commits a heedless Act, so that the Worship becomes invalid through something determinated, or who is in doubt and does not know whether he performed a Worship of three *rak'ahs* or four, in these cases begins with what he is sure about, and performs two Prostrations of Forgetfulness before the Salutation. And if he forgets then he performs them after the Salutation whenever he remembers after a short time. For if he performs a Prostration after the Salutation and after he has done something that invalidates his state of ceremonial cleanness, his Worship is invalid. For, after he enters upon the Prostration, it is as if he makes his Salutation out of place through forgetfulness, so validation does not result because of it and he may return to the Worship. So, for that reason, he makes a new Salutation after the Prostration. But if he remembers about the Prostration of Forgetfulness after leaving the mosque, or after a long period, it has escaped.

Another Problem. Evil Suggestion during the Intention to Perform the Worship. Its causes is unsoundness in the mind, or ignorance of the religious law. For, obedience to the command of Allah is like obedience to the command of anyone else, and magnifying His is like magnifying anyone else, so far as purpose is concerned. Anyone who has a learned man come to him rises for him. Then were he to say, "I have the intention to rise and stand, magnifying the entrance of the honourable Zaid, on account of his excellence, synchronising my action with his entrance, turning to him with my face," he would be weak-minded. Nay, but as he sees him, and becomes aware of his excellence, the impulse to magnify rises in him of itself, and makes him stand up, and he becomes a magnifier, except when he rises for some other occupation, or rises in a state of unmindfulness.

The Stipulation for the Worship to be "noon," "a regular payment," and "prescribed," so that the obedience may be complete, is like the stipulation for the standing of the host to be united with the entrance of the learned man, along with facing the one coming in, and along with the non-existence of any other motive but that, and united with the purpose of magnifying him by means of the standing up, in order that the standing up may be a magnifying. For, if he were to stand up, turning his back, or wait and then stand up after a while, he would not be a magnifier.

Next, these qualities must needs be known and intended by the worshipper. Next, there presence in the self does not occupy so long as a single moment, but only the setting in order of the expressions which indicate them is long, whether it be the utterance of them by the tongue or the thinking of them in the heart. So, whoever does not understand the Intention of the Worship after this sort, does not understand what intention is. For there is nothing more in it but that you were summoned to perform the Worship at a certain time, and you responded favourably and stood up to perform it. So, distraction through evil suggestions from Satan is sheer ignorance, for these purposes and these knowledges are united in the self in one state, and are not separated out into individual elements in the mind in such a way that the self may graze upon and consider them, for there is a difference between the presence of a thing in the self and differentiating it in the thought. Presence is the opposite of absence and unmindfulness, even though it is not differentiated. For, anyone who has knowledge of an originated thing, for instance, knows it in one knowledge and one state, but this knowledge includes knowledges which are present even though they are not differentiated. For, anyone who has knowledge of an originated thing has knowledge of the existent and the non-existent, and of coming before and coming after, and time, and knows that the coming before belongs to non-existence and coming after to existence. These knowledges are comprised under the knowledge of the originated thing, by the proof that anyone who has knowledge of an originated thing and has no further knowledge about it, and were he asked, "Did you know the coming before only, or the coming after, or non-existence, or the preceding of the non-existence, or the coming after of the existence, or time, which is divided into past and future?" should reply, "I have never known it," would be a liar, and his speech would be contradictory to his saying, "I know the originated thing."

From ignorance of this point distraction is aroused. Then indeed the distracted man imposes on himself the task of making present in his heart that it is a noontime act, and that it is a performance of a duty at its appointed time, and that it is prescribed, all in one state, differentiated into its various expressions while he observes them, which is absurd. Were he to impose that task on himself in standing up for a learned man, it would be impossible for him. So, by this knowledge, distraction is warded off, and it is simply that he knows that obedience to the command of Allah in the Intention is like obedience to the command of someone else.

Furthermore, I add to it, by way of facilitation and permission, and say, Were the one who is distracted not to understand what the Intention is without the presence of these things separately, and were he not to picture within himself the obedience of a single act, and were he to present the whole of that during the *takbir,* from its beginning to its end, so that he would not finish the *takbir* without having secured the Intention, he should let that suffice him. We would not burden him with the task of joining the whole to the beginning of the *takbir* or to the end of it, for that would be an excessive burden. Had that been commanded, a question about it would have occurred to the first believers, and one of the Companions would have been distracted in the Intention. So, the absence of the occurrence of that is a proof that the command is on an easy basis. Therefore, it is fitting that the one who is distracted should be content with whatever way is made easy for him, so that it may become habitual for him, and distraction may leave him. He should not demand of himself meticulous precision in that, for the effort to be precise increases distraction. We have mentioned in the *'Fatwas,*[236] aspects of the precise requirements in the analysis of the cognitions and purposes connected with the

236. 'This is a collection of 190 *fatwas,* and is mentioned in Sayyid Murtada, I, 42.

7

Supererogatory Performances of the Worship

Know that the performances of the Worship that are not *fard*, Prescribed, are divided into three parts: the *sunnah*, Usage, the *mustahabb*, Liked, and the *tatawwu'*, Voluntary.

We mean by the *sunnah*, Usage, those of which it is handed down from the Messenger of Allah that he consistently performed them, such as the *ratibah*, Fixed, performances following the *fard*, Prescribed, performances of the Worship; the *duha*, Forenoon, Worship; the *witr*, Odd, Worship, the *tahajjud*, Night, Worship and others, for the word *sunnah*, "usage", is an expression, of "the way that has been walked in".

We mean by the *mustahabb*, Liked, those whose excellence Tradition has reported, but the consistent performance of which has not been handed down, as we shall repeat in the Worship of the Days and Nights of the Week, and such as the Worship on going out of a dwelling, and entering it, and such like.

We mean by the *tatawwu'*, Voluntary, Worship those that come after that, which no tradition reports in particular, but which a creature does voluntarily, inasmuch as he is desirous of communion with Allah through a Worship whose excellence the religious law reports in a general way, and by which he shows himself to be free giver, since he was not urged to that Worship in particular, although he is urged to Worship in general, and *tatawwu'*, "Voluntary," is an expression for a gift freely given.

I have named the three divisions *nafl*, "Supererogatory," because "supererogatory" is "additional," and the whole of them are additional to the *fard*, Prescribed, performances of the Worship.

The expressions *nafilah*, "Supererogatory," *sunnah*, "Usage," *mustahabb*, "Liked," and *tatawwu'*, "Voluntary," we desired to use in a technical sense, to define these meanings, and it is no sin for anyone to change this technical use, and there is no strictness about the terms that may be used after their meanings are understood.

Each one of these three classes has degrees of excellence that differ from one another, in accordance with whatever any traditions and records say about them and their excellence, and in accordance with the duration of the continuance of the Messenger of Allah; and in accordance with the trustworthiness and repute of the traditions which have come down about them. For that reason it is said, "The Usages of the Congregational Worship are more excellent than the Usages of the individual Worship. The most excellent of the congregational Usages is the Worship of the Two Feasts; then the Eclipse of the Sun; then the Request for Rain. The most excellent of the individual Usages is the Odd Worship; then the two *rak'ahs* of the Dawn; then the Fixed Worship which comes after these two, according to their differences."

Know that the Supererogatory Worships, with regard to their connection with the circumstances on which they depend, are divided into: (a) those dependent upon causes, such as the Eclipse of the Sun, and the Request for Rain; (b) those dependent upon seasons. Those dependent upon seasons are divided into (1) what is repeated with the recurrence of day and night, or (2) with the recurrence of the week, or (3) with the recurrence of the year. In all, there are four classes.

Class One. Those that are Repeated with the Recurrence of the Days and Nights

These are eight in number. Five are the Fixed performances of the five Prescribed performances of the Worship, and three more after them are the Forenoon Worship, the Enlivening of what comes between the two Evening Worships and the Night Worship.

The first is the *ratibah*, Fixed, performance of the morning, which is of two *rak'ahs*. The Messenger of Allah said, "The two *rak'ahs* of the dawn are better than this life and what is in it." Its time begins with the appearance of the true dawn, which is that whereof the light spreads in the horizon, rather than the first or false dawn. The apprehension of that by the physical sight is difficult at the beginning of it, unless one learns the mansions of the moon or knows the conjuction of its appearance with the stars visible to the sight, and so deduces it from the stars. He may know it from the moon on two nights of the month, for the moon rises at dawn on the night of the twenty-sixth, and the morning appears at the setting of the moon on the night of the twelfth of the month. This is what is usual, but an irregularity enters it in some of the signs of the zodiac, and the explanation of that is lengthy. The learning of the mansions of the moon is one of the important duties of the devotee, so that he may observe by it the measurements of the times at night and in the morning.

The time of the two *rak'ahs* of the dawn elapses with the passing of the time of the Prescribed Worship of the morning, which is at the appearance of the sun. But the Usage is the payment of them before the Prescribed Worship. So, if one enters the mosque while the Worship has been instituted, let him engage in the Prescribed Worship, for Muhammad said, "Whenever the Worship is instituted, there is no Worship except the Prescribed." Then whenever he finishes the Prescribed, he stands up for those two *rak'ahs*, and performs them. The true view is that they are a payment so long as they occur before the appearance of the sun, for they follow upon the Prescribed Worship according to its time, and the order between them is a Usage in making one precede and the other follow only whenever he does not come upon a congregation. Whenever he does come upon a congregation, the order is reversed, but they remain a payment.

The liked thing is that he perform them at home, and be quick in them. Then he enters the mosque and performs the Worship of the two *rak'ahs* of the Greeting of the Mosque, and then sits down and does not perform a Worship until he performs the Prescribed Worship, During the time between the Morning Worship and the appearance of the sun the most liked thing is the *dhikr*, "invocation," and *fikr*, "meditation," and confining oneself to the two *rak'ahs* of the dawn and the Prescribed Worship.

The second is the Fixed Worship of noon, which consists of six *rak'ahs*; two come after the Noon Prescribed Worship, which is also a *sunnah muwakkadah*, "Confirmed Usage," and four come before it, which are also a Usage, although they are inferior to the two that come last. Abu Hurairah related from the Prophet that he said, "Whoever performs a Worship of four *rak'ahs* after the sun's passing the meridian, reciting well in them, and doing their Bowing and their Prostration well, has worshipping with him 70,000 angels, asking forgiveness for him until the night." Muhammad was wont not to miss four *rak'ahs* after the sun's passing the meridian, prolonging them, and said, "The doors of heaven are open at this hour, so I like some work to rise for me then." Abu Ayyub the Helper[238] related it, and was alone in handing it down. What Umm Habibah, the wife[239] of the Prophet, related, proved this also: "He said, 'Whoever performs every day a Worship of twelve *rak'ahs*, exclusive of the Prescribed, has built for him a house in the Garden; two *rak'ahs* before the Dawn Worship; four before the Noon; two *rak'ahs* after it; two *rak'ahs* before the Afternoon, and two after the Sunset Worships.' "

Ibn 'Umar said, "I have preserved from the Messenger of Allah 'on every day ten *rak'ahs*,'" and he mentioned what Umm Habibah mentioned, except the two *rak'ahs* of Dawn, for he said, "That was an hour in which the Messenger of Allah was wont not to be visited, but my sister, Hafsah,[240] has told me that he used to perform a Worship of two *rak'ahs* in her house and then go out." He said in his tradition, "Two *rak'ahs* before the Noon, and two *rak'ahs* after the Evening Worships." So two *rak'ahs* before the Noon have become better confirmed than the whole four.

The time of that begins with the passing of the meridian. The passing is known by the lengthening of the shadow of people standing erect, inclining to the direction of the east, since the shadow of a man falls to the side of the west at the appearing of the sun, being long. So the sun continues to rise, while the shadow grows less, and swerves from the direction of the west until the sun reaches the utmost degree of its elevation, this being the measure of midday, and that is the utmost degree of the

---

238. Abu Ayyub Khalid b. Zaid al-Ansari (d. 52 A.H.).

239. Umm Habibah, daughter of Abu Sufyan, and one of Muhammad's wives (d. 44 A.H.).

240. Hafsah, daughter of the Khalifah 'Umar, wife of Muhammad (d. 45 A.H.).

shortness of the shade. Then, when the sun passes from the utmost degree of elevation, the shadow begins to lengthen. Then whenever the increase becomes appreciable to the sense, the time of noon begins. One knows of a surety that the passing of the meridian according to the knowledge of Allah occurred before it, but duties are not connected with anything except what comes under the observation of the sense. The amount of the shade remaining, which is cast from a man, goes on increasing, being long in winter and short in summer. The utmost degree of its length is when the sun reaches the first of Capricorn, and the utmost degree of its shortness is at its reaching the first of Cancer. One may know that by means of perserverance and measurements. Of the methods at hand for making sure, for him who is excellent at taking observations of the stars, one is that he should note the axis of the north at night, and place upon the earth a square board in a symmetrical position, so that the one of its sides towards the polar-axis is in a position, so that if you were to suppose a stone fell from the axis to the earth, and then suppose a line were extended from the place where the stone fell to the side of the board which is near it, then the line would form upon the board two right angles, that is the line would not be inclining to either one of the two sides. Then you erect a post upon the board, vertically and symmetrically, in the place of the mark (o), which is opposite the polar-axis. Its shade falls upon the board at the first part of the day, inclining towards the direction of the west on the side of line (a). Then it continues to incline until it superimposes itself on line (b), so that, as it moves, could its end be extended, it would reach in a straight line to the place of the falling of the stone, and it would be parallel to the east and the west sides of the board, inclining to neither one of them. Then, when its inclination to the west side ceases, the sun reaches the utmost degree of its elevation, and then, when the shadow swerves from the line which is upon the board to the east side, the sun has passed the meridian. This is apprehended by the sense, giving

THE EAST SIDE

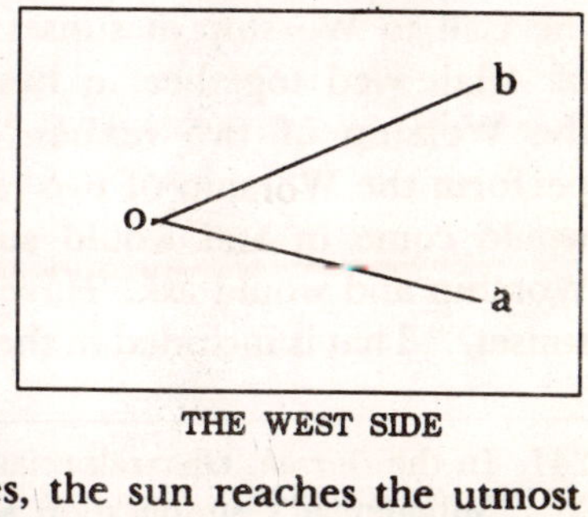

THE WEST SIDE

assurance of the time which is near to the beginning of the passing of the meridian as it is in the knowledge of Allah. Then you make a mark at the end of the shade when it swerves, and so, when the shadow from the mark becomes like the post itself in length, the time of *'asr*, mid-afternoon, begins. There is no harm in having this amount of knowledge of the passing of the meridian. As in drawing above.

The third is the Fixed Worship of mid-afternoon. It is four *rak'ahs* before the Mid-afternoon Worship. Abu Hurairah related from the Prophet that he said, "Allah has mercy upon any creature who performs a Worship of four *rak'ahs* before the Mid-afternoon Worship." So, doing that in the hope of participating in the request[241] of the Messenger of Allah is liked with a confirmed liking, for his request is certainly answered affirmatively. But his consistent performance of the Usage Worship before mid-afternoon was not like his consistent performance of the two *rak'ahs* before the Noon Worship.

The fourth is the *ratibah*, Fixed, Worship of sunset. It is two *rak'ahs* after the Prescribed Worship. The narratives do not agree about them. But as regards two *rak'ahs* before it, between the *mu'adhdhin's* Call to the Worship and the *mu'adhdhin's* Institution of the Worship, by way of losing no time, this has been handed' down from a company of the Companions, such as Ubayy b. Ka'b 'Abadah b. Samit,[242] Abu Dahrr and Zaid b. Thabit[243] and others. 'Abadah, or someone else, said, "Whenever the *mu'adhdhin* gave the Call to Worship at sunset the Companions of the Messenger of Allah vied together in hastening to the columns to perform the Worship of two *rak'ahs*." One of them said, "We used to perform the Worship of two *rak'ahs* before sunset so that someone would come in and would suppose that we had performed the Worship and would ask, 'Have you performed the Worship of the sunset?'" That is included in the general application of the statement

241. In the *Durrah,* Ghazzali relates a tradition that on Resurrection Day Muhammad's supplication will be: "My people! O my Lord! Give them peace!"

242. 'Abadah b. Samit (d. 34 A.H.).

243. Abu Sa'd Zaid b. Thabit b. al-Dahhak al-Ansari, Compiler of the Qur'an.

of Muhammad, "Between every two calls[244] to Worship there is a time of Worship, for whoever is willing." Ahmad b. Hanbal used to perform them and then the people remonstrated with him, so he abandoned them. Then he was asked about that, so he said, "I did not see the people performing them so I abandoned them." And he said, "If a man performs them in his house, or a place where the people would not see him, that would be well."

The time of the setting of the sun begins at the disappearance of the sun from the sight in level countries which are not encompassed by mountains. If they are encompassed by mountains in the direction of the west, one pauses until one sees the approach of darkness on the side of the east. Muhammad said, "Whenever night approaches from there and day departs from their, the one fasting enters upon the time of the breaking of the fast."

The most liked thing is to lose no time in performing the Worship of sunset especially. If you delay and perform the Worship before the disappearance of the red after-glow, it would be a payment of the Worship in the prescribed time, but it is disliked. 'Umar delayed the Worship of sunset one night until stars appeared, so he freed a slave. Ibn 'Umar delayed it until two stars appeared, so he freed two slaves.

The Fixed performance of the last Evening Worship is four *rak'ahs* after the Prescribed. Evening Worship. 'A'ishah said, "The Messenger of Allah used to perform a Worship of four *rak'ahs* after the last Evening Worship. We would then sleep."

Some of the learned chose from the whole body of the traditions to hold that the number of the *ratibah,* Fixed, Worships was seventeen, like the number of the Prescribed Worships: two before the Morning, four before the Noon, and two after it, four before the Afternoon, and two after the Sunset, and three after the last Evening Worship, this being the Odd Worship. When the traditions which have come down about this are known, there is no sense in conjecturing about it. For Muhammad has said, "The Worship is the best task, so whoever will does much, and whoever will does little."

---

244. The *adhan* Call, and *iqamah,* Institution, explains Sayyid Murtada.

So then the choice of every devotee from these Voluntary Worships is in the measure of his desire for good. So it has appeared in what we have mentioned that some of them are better confirmed than others, and to abandon the better confirmed ones is certainly less desirable. The Prescribed Worships are completed by the Supererogatory ones, and so to the one who does not seek much of them for himself it will soon happen that his Prescribed Worship will not be sound without a restorer.

The sixth is the *witr*, Odd, Worship. Anas b. Malik said, "The Messenger of Allah used to perform a *witr* Worship after the Evening Worship with three *rak'ahs*, reciting in the first, 'Say the Praise of the name of thy Lord Most High!' (Qur'an, ixxxvii.), and in the second, "Say, O ye Unbelievers' (cix.), and in the third, 'Say, He is Allah, One' (cxii.)."

It occurs in Tradition that Muhammad used to perform, after the *witr* Worship, a Worship of two *rak'ahs* in a sitting position, and in some of them it is said, "sitting cross-legged". In some traditions it is said, "When he wished to get into his bed, he dragged himself to it, and performed a Worship of two *rak'ahs* before he lay down, reciting in them, 'When the earth quakes' (xcix.), and Surat al-Takathur' (cii.), and in another account 'Say, O ye Unbelievers!' (cix.)."

The *witr* Worship is permissible unconnected and connected with one and two Salutations. The Messenger of Allah performed an Odd Worship with one and three and five, and so on, with odd numbers up to eleven *rak'ahs* (the narrative about thirteen is uncertain), and in an exceptional tradition, seventeen *rak'ahs*. These *rak'ahs*, I mean what we have called as a whole the *witr*, Odd, Worship, were Muhammad's Worship at night, and are the *tahajjud*, Night, Worship. The Night Worship is a confirmed *sunnah*, Usage, and its excellence will appear in the *Book of Wirds*, "Devotional Recitals".

With regard to the most excellent there is disagreement, for it is said, "To perform a single *rak'ahs* is more excellent. since, it is validated that Muhammad used to perform consistently the Odd Worship with a single *rak'ah.*"

It is said, "The connected *witr* Worship is more excellent to avoid the appearance of contradiction" (of the views of others).

Especially the *imam*, since one who does not consider that a single *rak'ah* is a Worship may sometimes be led by him, if he performs a connected Worship, should state the Intention of performing a *witr* Worship by means of the whole. If he confines himself to one *rak'ah* after the two *rak'ahs* of the *sunnah*. Evening Worship, or after the Prescribed Evening Worship, he states the Intention of performing the *witr* Worship, and it is valid, because the Stipulation of the *witr* Worship is that it should be in itself odd in number, and that it would make whatever else that went before it odd, and so, it would make the Prescribed Worship a *witr* Worship. Were he to perform the *witr* Worship before the Evening Worship it would not be valid, that is, would not secure the excellence of the *witr* Worship, which is better for him than the choice parts of the flock, as the tradition about it says. And if not, the single *rak'ah* is valid at whatever time it may be performed. It is not valid before the Evening Worship only because it violates the Agreement of the people concerning the act, and because what becomes a *witr* Worship by means of it does not precede it.

But whenever one wishes to perform a *witr* Worship of three *rak'ahs* unconnected with a *fard* or *sunnah* Worship,[245] consideration is in place in regard to the statement of his Intention about the two *rak'ahs*. For, if he states the Intention of performing, by means of them, *tahajjud* Night, Worship or the *sunnah*, Usage, Evening Worship, it would not be of the *witr* class. But, if he should state the Intention to perform the *witr* Worship, it would not in itself be a *witr* Worship for the *witr* Worship would be only what comes after it. But the most obvious thing is that he should state the Intention of the *witr* Worship in the three unconnected ones. But the *witr* Worship has two meanings: one of them is that it should in itself be odd in number, and the other is that it should begin to be made a *witr* Worship by what comes after it. So the total of the three would be a *witr* Worship, and the two *rak'ahs* would be part of the total of the three, except that its quality of being a *witr* Worship would depend upon the third *rak'ah*. If he resolves to make a *witr* Worship of the two of them, by means of a third, it is for him to state the Intention of Performing a *witr* Worship by means of them, for the third *rak'ah* is a *witr* in

245. Sayyid Murtada adds "and therefore with two Salutations."

itself, and is one that renders other than itself *witr*, while the two *rak'ahs* do not make others a *witr* and they are not in themselves *witr*, but they are made *witr* by others.

It is fitting that the *witr* Worship should be the last Worship of the night, so it occurs after the *tahajjud*, Night, Worship. The excellences of the *witr*, Odd, Worship and the *tahajjud*, Night, Worship and the manner of the order between the two of them will come in the *Book of the Order of the Wirds*, "Devotional Recitals."

The seventh is the *duha*, Forenoon, Worship. Now, consistent performance of this is one of the most dutiful and excellent of acts. As for the number of its *rak'ahs*, the most, in what is handed down about it, is eight *rak'ahs*. Umm Hani,[246] the sister of 'Ali b. Abu Talib, related that Muhammad performed a Forenoon Worship of eight *rak'ahs*, prolonging them and doing them well, but no one else has handed down this amount. But 'A'ishah has mentioned that Muhammad used to perform the Forenoon Worship with four *rak'ahs* and add whatever Allah willed that he should add. So, she did not prevent additional, that is, he used consistently to do four, and not less than that, and perhaps additional. It is related in a *mufrad* tradition, "with a single authority," that the Prophet used to perform the Forenoon Worship with six *rak'ahs*.

As for its time, 'Ali related that Muhammad used to perform the Forenoon Worship with six *rak'ahs* at two times: one, when the sun appears and advances he would get up and perform two *rak'ahs*, which is the first part of the second of the *wirds*. Portions, of the Day, as shall appear later.[247] When the sun brightens up and is in a fourth of the sky on the side of the east, he would perform four. But the first is whenever the sun mounts only the measure of half a lance, and the second is whenever a fourth of the day goes, in correspondence with the Afternoon Worship, for its time is when a fourth of the day remains. Noon is at the middle of the day, and the Forenoon Worship is at the middle point between the appearance of the sun and its passing the meridian, just as mid-afternoon is at the middle point between the passing

246. Umm Hani, sister of 'Ali b. Abu Talib, wife of Muhammad.
247. This is at Sayyid Murtada. V., 140 ff.

of the meridian and the setting of the sun. This is the most excellent of the times. From the time of the ascent of the sun until what comes before its passing of the meridian, is, in brief, a time for the Forenoon Worship.

The eighth is the Enlivening of what comes between the two Evening Worships, and this is a *sunnah muwakkadah*, Confirmed Usage. From what is on record concerning the practice of the Messenger of Allah between the two Evening Worships, its number is six *rak'ahs*. The Worship has great excellence. It is said, "It is what is referred to in the saying of Allah, 'Their sides withdraw from the couches' (xxxii. 16)." It has been related from Muhammad that he said, "Whoever performs Worship between the Sunset and the Evening performs one that is a Worship of 'those who return to Allah."[248] Muhammad said, "For him who secludes himself during the time between the Sunset and the Evening Worships in a congregational mosque, not speaking except in worship,[249] or in recital of the Qur'an, there is obligation on Allah to build in the Garden two palaces, the extent of each one of them being a hundred years' journey, and set out for him between them a plantation which would contain the people of this life walking about in it." The rest of its excellences will appear in the *Book of the Wirds*, "Devotional Portions," if Allah will.

Class Two. Those That are Repeated with the Recurrence of the Weeks

These are the performances of the Worship of the days and nights of the weeks, for every day and every night.

(a) As for the days, we will begin in them with Sunday.

(1) *Sunday*. Abu Hurairah related from the Prophet that he said, "Whoever performs a Worship of four *rak'ahs* on Sunday, reciting in each *rak'ah* the Fatihat al-Kitab (i.) and the verses beginning 'The Messenger believed' (ii. 285) once, has Allah write for him good deeds according to the number of all the Christians, men and women, and Allah gives him the reward of a Prophet,

---

248. The reference is to Qur'an, xvii. 26-27.

249. Sayyid Murtada defines *al-salah* here as simply *al-du'a'*, "Supplication".

and records for him a Pilgrimage and minor visit to the Ka'bah, and records for him in every *rak'ah* a thousand Worships, and Allah gives him in the Garden for every consonant a city of excellent musk."

It is related from 'Ali b. Abu Talib from the Prophet that he said, "Assert belief in the unity of Allah with much Worship on the One Day,[250] for Allah is One, and has no associate, for whoever performs a Worship on Sunday, after the Noon Worship, of four *rak'ahs* after the Prescribed and the Usage *rak'ahs*, reciting in the first, the Fatihat al-Kitab (i.), and 'The Sending[251] Down of the Book of the Surat al-Sajdah' (xxxii.), and 'He is blessed in whose hand is the Dominion' (lxvii.), and then gives the Witness and the Salutation, and then stands up and performs the Worship of the other two *rak'ahs*, reciting in them the Fatihat al-Kitab (i.), and Surat al-Jumu'ah (lxii), and makes a request of Allah for what he needs has a right upon Allah to satisfy his need."

(2) *Monday*. Jabir[252] related from the Messenger of Allah that he said, "Whoever performs a Worship on Monday at the advance of the day, of two *rak'ahs*, reciting in each *rak'ah* the Fatihat al-Kitab (i.) once and the Throne Verse (ii. 256) once, and 'Say, He is Allah, One' (cxii.), and the two Seekings for Refuge (cxiii., cxiv.) once each, and then, when he says the Salutation, says the Seeking of Forgiveness ten times, and says the Blessing upon the Prophet ten times, has Allah forgive him his sins, all of them."

Anas b. Malik related from the Prophet that he said, "Whoever performs a Worship on Monday of twelve *rak'ahs*, reciting in every *rak'ah* the Fatihat al-Kitab (i.) and the Verse of the Throne (ii. 256) once, and then, when he finishes, recites, 'Say, He is Allah, One' (cxii.) twelve times, and says the Seeking of Forgiveness twelve times, will be called on Resurrection Day: "Where is Such a one, son of Such a one? Let him stand! and let him take his reward from Allah." Then the first reward given will be a thousand robes, and he will be crowned and it will be said to him,

250. This is the name of Sunday in Arabic.
251. There are five other *surahs*, that begin with *tanzil*, "sending down," viz. xxxix. xl., xli., xlv. and xlvi.
252. Jabir b. 'Abdallah the Helper (d. 74 A.H.).

'Enter the Garden!' Then there will meet him a hundred thousand angels, each angel with a gift, escorting him so that he visits in turn a thousand palaces of light, shining brightly."

(3) *Tuesday.* Yazid al-Raqashi related from Anas b. Malik that he said, "Muhammad said, 'Whoever performs on Tuesday a Worship of ten *rak'ahs,* at the middle of the day,' and in another tradition, 'at the advance of the day, reciting in each *rak'ah* the Fatihat al-Kitab (i.) and the Verse of the Throne (ii. 256) once, and, 'Say, He is Allah, One' (cxii.) three times, does not have a sin recorded against him for seventy days, and if he dies up to seventy days, he dies a martyr, and is forgiven the sins of seventy years."

(4) *Wednesday.* Abu Idris al-Khawlani[253] related from Ma'adh b. Jabal that he said, "The Messenger of Allah said, 'Whoever performs a Worship on Wednesday of twelve *rak'ahs* at the advance of the day, reciting in each *rak'ah* the Fatihat al-Kitab (i.) and the Verse of the Throne (ii. 256) once, and "Say, He is Allah, One" (cxii.) three times, and the two Seekings for Refuge (cxiii., cxiv.) three times, has an angel call him at the Throne, "O 'Abdallah! begin the work anew, for Allah has forgiven you whatever sins have gone before, and Allah has removed from you the punishment of the grave as well as its straitness and its darkness, and has removed from you the hardships of the Resurrection," and there is sent up for him for that day the work of a Prophet.'"

(5) *Thursday.* From 'Ikrimah from Ibn 'Abbas it is related that he said, "The Messenger of Allah said, 'Whoever performs a Worship of two *rak'ahs* on Thursday, between the Noon and the Afternoon Worships, reciting in the first the Fatihat al Kitab (i.) once, and the Verse of the Throne (ii. 256) a hundred times, and in the second the Fatihat al-Kitab once, and, "Say, He is Allah, One" (cxii.) a hundred times, and recites the Blessing upon Muhammad a hundred times, has Allah give him the reward of one who fasts the three months of Rajab, Sha'ban and Ramadan, and he has the reward like that of a pilgrim to the House, and has written for him good deeds according to the number of everyone who believes in Allah and trusts Him.'"

---

253. Abu Idris al-Khawlani (d. 80 A.H.).

(6) *Friday.* It is related from 'Ali b. Abu Talib from the Prophet that he said, "Friday is a Worship in its totality. There is no believing creature who gets up when the sun rises and advances the measure of a lance or more than that and then performs the ablution well, and then performs the Worship of Praise of the forenoon with two *rak'ahs*, with faith and belief, but has Allah record for him two hundred good deeds, and erase from him two hundred evil deeds, and whoever performs a Worship of four *rak'ahs* has Allah exalt him four hundred degrees in the Garden, and whoever performs eight *rak'ahs* has Allah exalt him in the Garden eight hundred degrees and forgive him his sins, all of them, and whoever performs twelve *rak'ahs* has Allah record for him two thousand and two hundred good deeds and erase from him two thousand and two hundred evil deeds, and has Allah exalt him in the Garden two thousand and two hundred degrees."

From Nafi' from Ibn 'Umar from the Prophet it is related that he said, "Whoever enters the congregational mosque on Friday and then performs a Worship of four *rak'ahs* before the Worship of the Friday Observance, reciting in every *rak'ah* the Praise (i.), and, 'Say, He is Allah, One' (cxii.) fifty times, will not die until he sees his place of sitting of the Garden or it is seen for him."

(7) *Saturday.* Abu Hurairah related that the Prophet said, "Whoever performs a Worship on Saturday of four *rak'ahs,* reciting in each *rak'ah* the Fatihat al-Kitab once and, 'Say, He is Allah, One,' three times, and, when he finishes, recites the Verse of the Throne (ii. 256), has Allah record for him, for every consonant, a Pilgrimage, and minor visit to the Ka'bah and raise up for him the reward of a year of fasting during its days, and of standing for Worship during its nights and has Allah give him for every consonant the reward of a martyr, and he is under the shade of the Throne of Allah with the Prophets and martyrs."

(b) As for the nights.

(1) *The Eve of Sunday.* Anas b. Malik related concerning the eve of Sunday that Muhammad said, "Whoever performs a Worship on the eve of Sunday of twenty *rak'ahs* reciting in every *rak'ah* the Fatihat al-Kitab (i.) and, 'Say, He is Allah, One' (cxii.) fifty times, and the two Seekings for Refuge (cxiii. cxiv.) each once,

and says the Seeking of Forgiveness of Allah a hundred times, and says the Seeking of Forgiveness for himself and for his parents a hundred times, and says the Blessing upon the Prophet a hundred times, and renounces[254] his claiming of any power and strength, and seeks the protection of Allah, and then says, 'I bear witness that there is no god but Allah, and I bear witness that Adam is the sincere friend of Allah and His original formation, and Ibrahim is the cordial friend of Allah, and Moses is the interlocutor of Allah, and 'Isa is the Spirit of Allah, and Muhammad is the beloved of Allah,', has reward in accordance with the number of those who assert Allah has a son, and those who do not assert that Allah has a son, and Allah raises him along with the faithful on Resurrection Day, and he has a right upon Allah to admit him into the Garden with the Prophets."

(2) *The Eve of Monday.* Al-A'mash[255] related from Anas b. Malik that he said, "The Messenger of Allah said, 'Whoever performs a Worship on the eve of Monday, with four *rak'ahs,* reciting in the first the "Praise belongs to Allah" (i.) and, "Say, He is Allah, One" (cxii.) ten times, and in the second, the "Praise belongs to Allah," and "Say, He is Allah One" twenty times, and in the third the "Praise belongs to Allah," and, "Say, He is Allah, One" thirty times, and in the fourth, the Praise belongs to Allah," and, "Say, He is Allah, One" forty times, and then says the Salutation, and recites, "Say, He is Allah, One" seventy-five times, and says the Seeking of Forgiveness of Allah for himself and his parents seventy-five times, and then makes his request of Allah, has a right upon Allah to give him his request that he asked.'" This is called "the Worship of Need"

(3) *The Eve of Tuesday.* "Whoever performs a Worship of two *rak'ahs,* reciting in each *rak'ah* the Fatihat al-Kitab and 'Say, He is Allah, One,' and the two Seekings for Refuge (cxiii., cxiv.)., fifteen times, and recites, after the saying of the Salutation, fifteen times, the Verse of the Throne (ii. 256) and says the Seeking of Forgiveness of Allah fifteen times, has great reward, and substantial recompense."

It is related from 'Umar from the Prophet, that he said,

---

254. That is, by saying, "There is no power and no strength but in Allah."
255. Abu Muhammad Sulaiman b. Mihran al-A'mash (d. 148 A.H.).

"Whoever performs a Worship on the eve of Tuesday, with two *rak'ahs,* reciting in each *rak'ah* the Fatihat al-Kitab once, and 'Verily, We sent it down' (xcvii), and, 'Say, He is Allah, One,' seven times, has Allah free his neck from the Fire, and on Resurrection Day, be his leader and guide into the Garden."

(4) *The Eve of Wednesday.* Fatimah related from the Prophet, that he said, "For everyone who, on the eve of Wednesday, performs a Worship of two *rak'ahs,* reciting in the first the Fatihat al-Kitab once, and, 'Say, I seek refuge in the Lord of the dawn' (cxiii.) ten times, and in the second, the Fatihat al-Kitab once, and, 'Say, I seek refuge in the Lord of mankind' (cxiv.) ten times, then, after the Salutation, says the Seeking of Forgiveness of Allah ten times, and says the Blessing upon Muhammad ten times, there will descend from every heaven seventy thousand angels, recording his reward until the Day of Resurrection."

In another tradition, "Sixteen *rak'ahs,* reciting after the Fatihah whatever Allah may will, and reciting in the last two *rak'ahs* the Verse of the Throne thirty times, and in the first two thirty times, Say, He is Allah, One,' he intercedes for ten of the people of his household, all of whom deserve the Fire."

Fatimah is related to have said, "Muhammad said, 'Whoever, on the eve of Wednesday, performs a Worship of six *rak'ahs,* reciting in every *rak'ah* after the Fatihah, "Say, O Allah, Possessor of the Dominion" (iii. 25) to the end of the verse, and when he finishes his Worship, says, "May Allah requite Muhammad his desert in our behalf," has forgive him the sins of seventy years, and has recorded for him freedom from the Fire.' "

(5) *The Eve of Thursday.* Abu Hurairah said, "The Messenger of Allah said, "Whoever, on the eve of Thursday, between the Sunset and the Evening Worships, performs a Worship of two *rak'ahs,* reciting in each *rak'ah* the Fatihat al-Kitab and the Verse of the Throne five times, and "Say, He is Allah, One" five times, and then, when he finishes his Worship, says the Seeking of Forgiveness of Allah fifteen times, and puts his reward to the credit of his parents, repays the right of his parents upon him, even though he was undutiful to them, and Allah gives him what is given the righteous and the martyrs.' "

(6) *The Eve of Friday.* Jabir said, "The Messenger of Allah said, 'Whoever, on the eve of Friday, between the Sunset and the Evening Worships, performs, a Worship of twelve *rak'ahs,* reciting in every *rak'ah* the Fatihat al-Kitab once and, "Say, It is! Allah is One!" eleven times, is regarded as if he had performed a creature's service to Allah for twelve years, fasting all its days and standing for Worship all its nights.' "

Anas said, "The Prophet said,'Whoever performs, on the eve of Friday, the last Evening Worship in the congregation, and performs the Worship of the two *rak'ahs* of the *sunnah,* Usage, and then performs after them a Worship of ten *rak'ahs,* reciting in every *rak'ah* the Praise (i.) and "Say, He is Allah, One" (cxii,) and the two Seekings for Refuge (cxiii, cxiv.) each once, and then performs a *witr,* Odd, Worship of three *rak'ahs,* and then sleeps on his right side with his face toward the *qiblah,* will have it as if he had enlivened the Night of Decree.'"

Muhammad said, "Do much of the Asking of Blessing on me on the Night of Eager Desire and the Day of Brightness, that is, on the eve of Friday and on Friday."

(7) *The eve of Saturday.* Anas said, "The Messenger of Allah said, 'Whoever, on the eve of Saturday, between the Sunset and the Evening Worships, performs a Worship of twelve *rak'ahs,* has built for him a palace in the Garden, and it is as if he has given alms to every believer, man and woman, and is innocent of Judaism, and has a right[256] upon Allah to forgive him.' "

Class Three. Those Performances of Worship that are Repeated with the Recurrence of Years

There are four of this class: the Worship of the Two Feasts, the *tarawih,* "rest-giving," Worship of Ramadan, the Worship of Rajab and the Worship of the middle of Sha'ban.

(a) The first is the Worship of the Two Feasts. It is a *sunnah muwakkadah,* Confirmed Usage, and one of the distinctive rites of al-Islam. It is fitting that seven things should be observed in it.

The first is that the *takbir* is in series of three, so he say, "Allah

---

256. Sayyid Murtada explains this as "by way of the favour and grace of Allah."

is greater! Allah is greater! Allah is greater indeed!" and "Much praise belongs to Allah," and "Praise belongs to Allah morning and evening! There is no god but Allah only! He has no associate! we devote to Him our religion sincerely; even though the unbelievers disapprove!"

One begins with the *takbir* on the eve of the Feast of the Breaking of the Fast of the Ramadan until the beginning upon the Worship of the Feast. In the second Feast he begins the *takbir* after the morning of the Day of 'Arafah until the end of the day of the thirteenth, and this is the most perfect of the statements. He repeats the *takbir* after the Prescribed Worship and after the Supererogatory Worship, the one after the Prescribed being better confirmed.

The second is that when he gets up on the morning of the day of the Feasts, he bathes and adorns and perfumes himself, as we have mentioned regarding the Friday Observance. The cloak and the turban are most excellent for men, and let boys avoid silk, and the aged adornment, on going out.

The third is that he leaves one way and returns another. So did the Messenger of Allah. Muhammad used to command the unmarried girls and those who wore veils to be sent out.

The fourth is that it is liked to go out to the desert, except in Mecca and Jerusalem. But if it should be a rainy day, there is no objection to Worship in the mosque. It is permissible on a clear day for the *imam* to command a man to perform the Worship with those who are unable to go out in the mosque and himself go out with the able, saying the *takbir* on the way.

The fifth is that he observes the time. For the time of the Worship of the Feasts is between the rising of the sun and its passing the meridian, and the time of slaughtering for the sacrifices is after the rising of the sun and the length of time it takes for two addresses and two *rak'ahs* until the close of the thirteenth day. It is liked to hasten the Worship of the *adha*, Sacrifices, on account of slaughtering, and to delay the Worship of the Breaking of the Fast, for the sake of distributing the alms of the *fitr*, Breaking of the Fast, before the Worship, This is a Usage of the Messenger of Allah.

The sixth is about the manner of the Worship. Let the people go out saying the *takbir* on the way, and when the *imam* reaches the place of Worship, he should not sit down and should not perform any *nafilah* Worship. The people have the right to perform *nafilah* Worship.[257] Then the crier should cry, "The Worship is gathering!" The *imam* leads them with a Worship of two *rak'ahs*, saying the *takbir* in the first, except the *takbirat al-ihram* and of the Bowing, seven times, saying between every two *takbirs*, "O the Praise of Allah," and "The Praise belongs to Allah!" and "Allah is greater!" and says, "I have turned my face toward Him Who originally divided the heavens and the earth!" after the *takbir* of the Opening of the Worship. He should postpone the Seeking of Refuge until after the eighth *takbir* and recite Surah Qaf (i.) in the first *rak'ah* after the Fatihah and recite "The Hour drew near!" (liv.) in the second *rak'ah*. The extra *takbirs* in the second are five in number, apart from the *takbir* of the Standing Posture and the Bowing, and between every two *takbirs* are what we have mentioned. Then he gives the two addresses, sitting down between them. He whom the Worship of the Feast escapes performs a Substitute for it.

The seventh is that he sacrifices a sheep. The Messenger of Allah sacrificed two fine sheep, and slaughtered them with his own hand, and said, "In the name of Allah,"[258] and "Allah is greater! This is for me and any of my people who does not sacrifice!" Muhammad said, "Whoever sees the crescent of the moon of the month of Dhu al-Hijjah, and desires to sacrifice, should not take off any of his hair or finger nails." Abu Ayyub the Helper said, "A man used to sacrifice, in the time of the Messenger of Allah, a ewe, for the sake of his household and they used themselves to eat and to feed others." One has the right to eat from the sacrifice after three days and more. The permission for it came after the prohibition of it.

Sufyan al-Thawri said, "It is liked for one to perform a Worship, after the Feast of the Breaking of the Fast, of twelve

---

257. The other texts read "the people should stop performing the *nafilah* Worship."

258. Note that "the Merciful and Compassionate" is omitted on this occasion.

rak'ahs, and after the Feast of the Sacrifice, of six *rak'ahs*," and he said. "It is one of the Usages."

(b) The second is the *tarawih*, Rest-giving, Worship of Ramadan. It consists of twenty *rak'ahs*. The manner of performing it is well known. It is a Confirmed Usage, although it is inferior to the Worship of the Two Feasts. There is disagreement as to whether congregational or individual Worship is more excellent in this Worship. The Messenger of Allāh went to it two or three nights in the congregation. Then he did not go out, and said, "I fear that it may be made obligatory upon you." 'Umar gathered the people to it in congregation, inasmuch as it was safe from becoming obligatory through the cessation of the revelation. So it was said, "The congregational observance of it is more excellent because of the action of 'Umar, and because congregating together is a blessing and has excellence, as is evidenced by the Prescribed Observances, and because one, perhaps, would be lazy alone, and be zealous under the observation of a congregation."

It is also said, "The performances of it alone is more excellent because this is a *sunnah*, Usage that is, not one of the Rites of the Religion, like the Two Feasts." So its affiliation with the Worship of the Forenoon and the Greeting of the mosque is preferable, seeking that (a) congregational observance has not been made a law in them, and (b) that the custom has come to be that a group enters a mosque together and yet they do not perform the Worship of the Greeting of the Mosque in congregation, and (c) on account of the saying of Muhammad, "The superiority of the Voluntary Worship over the Worship in the mosque is like the superiority of the performance of the *maktub*, Prescribed, Worship in the mosque over the performance of the Worship in the house."

It is related that Muhammad said, "Worship in this my mosque (in Medina) is more excellent than a thousand performances of Worship in any other mosque, and Worship in the inviolate mosque (in Mecca) is more excellent than a thousand performances of the Worship in my mosque, and, more excellent than all of that, is the Worship of a man who performs in the corner of his house a Worship of two *rak'ahs* that no one knows about except Allah." This is because hypocrisy and affectation perhaps draw near to one in a congregation, and one is in safety against it alone. So this is what is said about it, and the preferred conclusion is that the congregational observance is more excellent as 'Umar considered. In some of the *nafilah* Worships congregational observance was made the law, and this Worship is worthy to be among the rites of the religion that are apparent.

As for taking account of hypocrisy in a congregation, and laziness when alone, this is turning aside from the consideration purposed in the excellence of the congregation, in so far as it is a congregational Worship. It is as though he who holds that position were saying, "The Worship is better for one than abandoning it, out of laziness," and "Singleness of devotion is better than hypocrisy." So, let us consider the question in the case of him who has confidence in himself, that he will not be lazy, even though he is by himself, and will not be hypocritical, even though he is present with a congregation, and, then, which of them is more excellent? In that case the opinion will turn between the blessing in a congregation, and the increase of the strength of one's singleness of devotion and presence of the heart when by oneself. So it is permissible that there should be some hesitancy with regard to the superiority of one of them over the other.

Among the acts that are liked there is *qunut*, Supplication, in the *witr* Worship in the latter half of Ramadan.

(c) As for the Worship of Rajab, it has been related *isnadan*, with a "traced" chain of witnesses, from the Messenger of Allah, that he said, "There is no one who fasts the first Thursday in Rajab and then performs a Worship between the first Evening Worship and the nightfall, of twelve *rak'ahs*, separating every two *rak'ahs* with a Salutation, reciting in each *rah'ah* the Fatihat al-Kitab once, and, 'Truly, We sent it down on the Night of Decree' (xcvii.) three times, and, 'Say, He is Allah, One" (cxii.) twelve times, and then, when he finishes his Worship, asks the Blessing for me seventy times, saying, 'O Allah, bless Muhammad, the unlettered Prophet, and his family!' and then performs a Prostration, and, while in prostration say, 'Praiseworthy, Holy, Lord of the angels and the spirit!' and then raises his head and says, seventy times, 'O Lord,! forgive and have mercy and pass over what Thou knowest! Verily Thus art the Most Mighty and the Most Wise and Kind!' and then performs another Prostration and says in it what is similar to that which he said in the first Prostration, and then makes request for what he needs, in his Prostration, but will have it performed."

Muhammad said, "There is no one who performs this Worship without having Allah forgive all his sins, even though they are like the froth of the sea, and the number of the sand, and the weight of the mountains, and the leaves of the trees, and there shall be intercession on behalf of seven hundred of his household of those who have deserved the Fire."

So, this Worship is liked, and we have set it forth in this section only because it is repeated with the recurrence of the years, although its degree does not approximate the degree of the Rest-giving Worship and the Worship of the Two Feasts, because a single line of authority (*ahad*) has handed this Worship down. But I saw the people of Jerusalem, all of them, consistently perform it, and not allow it to be abandoned, so I desired to set it forth.

(d) As for the Worship of Sha'ban. On the eve of the fifteenth of this month one performs a Worship of a hundred *rak'ahs*, every two *rak'ahs* with a Salutation reciting in every *rak'ah* after the Fatihah, "Say, He is Allah, One," eleven times, and, if he will, he performs ten *rak'ahs*, reciting in each *rak'ah* after the *Fatihah* one hundred times, "Say He is Allah, One," for this also is related in the totality of the performance of the Worship. The Fathers used to perform this Worship, and call it the "Good Worship," and gather together for it, and perhaps they performed it in congregation. It is related from al-Hasan that he said, "Thirty of the Companions of the Prophet reported to me that whoever performs this Worship on this night has Allah look upon him seventy times, and performs for him with each look seventy needs, the least of which is forgiveness."

Class Four. The Nafilah, Supererogatory, Worships that Depend upon Occasional Clauses, and Do not Depend upon Appointed Times

These are nine in number: the Worship of the Eclipse[259] of the

259. Sayyid Murtada (III, 427C) lists five different interpretations of *kusuf* and *khusuf: kusuf* is the change to blackness, while *khusuf* is the decrease of blackness; (2) both apply to the departure of light

Moon, and of the Eclipse of the Sun, of the Request for Rain, of the Greeting of the Mosque, the Two Rak'ahs between the Call to Worship and the Institution of the Worship, the Two *Rak'ahs* upon leaving the house and entering it, and the like. So we will mention those of them that occur to us now.

The first is the Worship of the Eclipse. The Messenger of Allah said, "The sun and the moon are two of the signs of Allah; they do not come into eclipse on account of the death or of the life of anyone, so whoever you see that, seek refuge in fear to the remembrance of Allah and to Worship." He said that when his boy Ibrahim died while the sun was in eclipse, and the people thereupon said, "It was in eclipse only on account of his death."

Consideration will now be given to its manner and its time. As for the manner, whenever the sun is in eclipse, in a time when the Worship is disliked or not disliked, there should be a Call to Congregational Worship, and the *imam* should lead the people in a Worship of two *rak'ahs* and bow in each *rak'ah* two times, with the former of both of them longer than the latter, of them, but he should not speak audibly. He recites in the first *rak'ah*, from the Standing Posture of the first *rak'ah*, the Fatihah and "The Cow" (ii.), and in the second, the Fatihah and "The Family of 'Imran' (iii.), and in the third, the Fatihah and "The Women" (iv.), and in the fourth, the Fatihah and "The Table" (v.), or that amount of the Qur'an, from whatever place he wishes. Were he to confine himself to the Fatihah in each *rak'ah*, that would suffice him. Were he to confine himself to the short *surahs*, there would be no harm, because the purpose of the prolongation is the continuance of the Worship until the clearance of the sun or moon after the eclipse. He says, "The Praise" in the first to the amount of a hundred verses, and in the second to the amount of eighty verses, and in the third to the amount of seventy verses, and in the fourth in the amount of fifty verses.

---

from the sun and moon, with *kusuf* at its beginning and with *khusuf* at its end; (3) *kusuf* applies to the departure of all the light, with *kusuf* for departure of part of the light; (4) *khusuf* for the departure of all the colour, with *kusuf* for the change of all the colour; (5) is the application of *kusuf* to the sun and *khusuf* to the moon.

Let the Prostration be equal to the length of the Bowing in each *rak'ah*. Then he delivers two addresses after the Worship, with a period of sitting between them. He commands the people to give alms, to free slaves, and to repent.

He does likewise in the eclipse of the moon, only in it he speaks audibly since it is at night.

As for the time, it is at the beginning of the eclipse until the completion of the clearance. The time for it also ends when the sun sets while in eclipse. The Worship of the Eclipse of the Moon passes when the dish of the sun appears, since it cancels the dominion of the night, but it does not pass with the setting of the moon. But if it clears in the midst of the Worship, one completes it quickly. Whoever overtakes the second Bowing with the *imam* has that *rak'ah* escape him, for the fundamental thing is the first Bowing.

The second is the Worship of the Petition for Rain. So, when the streams are lost in the earth, and the rains are cut off, or a canal collapses, it is liked for the *imam* to command the people first to fast three days, and do what they are able in giving alms, and to cease from unjustices, and to repent from disobedience, and then go out with them on the fourth day, along with the aged and the youths, all having cleansed themselves, in shabby and humble clothes, humbling themselves, in contrast to the feast days. It is said, "It is liked to take out the animals, because of their sharing the need, and because of the saying of Muhamamd, 'Were it not for the young nursing, and the elders bowing and the cattle feeding, there would surely be poured upon you punishment.' "

Were the non-Muslim people[260] under Muslim authority also to go out, distinguished by their marks, they should not be prohibited. Then, when they have all gathered together at the spacious place of Worship in the plain, the Call to Congregational Worship is given. When the *imam* performs a Worship of two *rak'ahs* with them, like the Worship of the two Feasts, without the

---

260. The *ahl al-dhimmah* are the people of a conquered country who do not embrace Islam are not enslaved, but are guaranteed life, liberty and modified property rights, with certain duties towards Muslims.

takbir. Then he delivers two addresses, with a brief sitting between them, and lets the Seeking for Refuge be the main part of the two addresses. It is fitting that, in the middle of the second address he should turn his back to the people and face the *qiblah*, and turn his cloak upside down at this time, drawing a good omen from the changing of the state. So did the Messenger of Allah. So he makes its upper part become the lower part, and what was on the right side appear on the left side, and what was on the lift side appear on the right side. So shall the people do.

Then they make a Supplication at this time inaudibly. Then the *imam* faces them and makes the address. They leave their cloaks turned as they were until they take them off when they take off their clothes. He says, in the supplication, "O Allah, Thou hast commanded us to make Supplication to Thee, and hast promised Thine answer: so we have Supplicated Thee, as Thou hast commanded us, and now answer us as Thou hast commanded us! O Allah, bestow upon us forgiveness of what we have committed, and Thine answer in providing us water, and in abundance of our apportioned sustenance." There is no harm in making supplication at the various performances of Worship during the three days preceding the going out. This Supplication has Proprieties and inward Stipulations, consisting of repentance and the restitution of wrongs, and of other things, and that will follow in the Book of *Da'awat*, Supplications.

The third is the Worship at Funerals. Its manner is well known. The most comprehensive Supplication handed down is what is related in the *Sahih* of al-Bukhari from 'Awf b. Malik.[261] He said, "I saw the Messenger of Allah perform a Worship at a funeral and I preserved this much of his supplication, 'O Allah, forgive him, have mercy on him, preserve him, pardon him, make his descent honourable, enlarge his entrance, wash him in water and snow and hail, cleanse him from sins, as one cleans a white garment of defilement, and change him to an abode better than his present abode, to a family better than his present family, and a mate better than his present make. Place him in the Garden and rescue him from the punishment of the Grave, and from the

---

261. 'Awf b. Malik al-Ashja' i (d. 73 A.H.).

punishment of the Fire!' so that," said 'Awf, "I desired that I were myself that dead man."

It is fitting that one who overtakes the second *takbir* should observe the Order of the Worship by himself, and say the *takbirs,* with the *takbirs* of the *imam,* and when the *imam* says the Salutation, he should perform a substitute for the *takbir* which escaped him, as is done by one late, for, were he to get ahead in saying the *takbirs* there would not remain any meaning to the imitation of the *imam* on the part of the worshipper in this Worship, since the *takbirs* are the apparent Elements, and worthy to have the standing of the *rak'ahs* in the rest of the Worships. This is to me the best regarded view, although some other than this is possible. The traditions that have appeared regarding the excellence of the Worship at funerals and the escorting of them are well known, so we will not be long by setting them forth. How should its excellence not be great, since it is one of the *fard kifayah* Worships, i.e. of general obligation, and since it becomes supererogatory only to him for whom it does not become *fard 'ain,* i.e. a personal obligation, through the presence of someone else. So then, one obtains by it the excellence of a *fard kifayah* Worship, although it is not a *fard 'ain* only because they altogether have undertaken to perform what is of general obligation, and thereby have removed the guilt of neglect from others. So that is not like a Supererogatory Worship which does not remove a Prescribed duty from anyone.

The desire for a great congregation is liked, seeking blessing by means of a great number of solicitudes and supplications, and because of its possible inclusion of someone whose supplication is answered, in accordance with what *Kuraib*[262] related from Ibn 'Abbas, to the effect that a son of his died, so he said, "O Kuraib, see how many men have gathered together for him." He said, "So I went out and, behold, many men had gathered together for him, so I told him. So he said, 'Would you say they are forty?' I said, 'Yes.' He said, 'Take him out then, for I heard the Messenger of Allah say, "No Muslim dies with forty men, who do not make anything to be an associate with Allah, performing

262. Abu Rishdin Kuraib b. Abu Muslim al-Hijazi (d. 98 A.H.).

the Worship of his funeral, but Allah welcomes their intercession for him." "

When he escorts the funeral and reaches the cemetery or enters it, at first he says, "The Peace is upon you O people of these abodes, of the believers and Muslims, and may Allah have mercy upon those who are coming later, for we, if Allah will, are to meet you!"

It is preferable that he should not depart until the dead man is buried. Then, when the grave is made over the dead man, he stands near it and says, "O Allah, Thy creature has returned to Thee, so have mercy upon him, and show mercy to him! O Allah, remove the earth from his two sides, and open the gates of heaven to his spirit, and receive him unto Thyself with a beautiful welcome, and, if he is a well-doer, double for him his good deeds; and, if he is an evil-doer, pass by his evil deeds."

The fourth: the Greeting of the Mosque is a Worship of two *rak'ahs* and more. It is a Confirmed Usage, so that it does not fall away, even though the *imam* is making the address on Friday, and the obligation of listening to the speaker is itself Confirmed. If he occupies himself with a Prescribed Worship, or performs a Substitution Worship that is due from him, the Worship of Greeting is thereby performed, and he gets the reward, since the purpose is that the beginning of his entrance should not be without the religious service especially belonging to the mosque, so performing the right of the mosque.

For this reason it is disliked for him to enter a mosque without having performed the ablution. So, if he enters to cross over or sit down, let him say, "Oh, the Praise of Allah!" and "Praise belongs to Allah!" and "There is not god but Allah!" and "Allah is greater!" saying them four times. It is said that they equal two *rak'ahs* in excellence.

The school of al-Shafi'i holds that the Greeting is not disliked in the times when the Worship ordinarily is disliked, which are (1) after mid-afternoon, (2) after the morning, (3) at the passing of the meridian, (4) at the rising, and (5) at the setting of the sun, in accordance with the tradition that is related, that Muhammad performed a Worship of two *rak'ahs* after mid-afternoon, and he was asked, "Did you not forbid us to do that?" So he said, "They are two *rak'ahs* that I was wont to perform afternoon, and the deputation preoccupied me from them."

This tradition provides two lessons. One of them is that dislike is limited to Worship that has no cause. The weakest of causes is performing Substitutions of *nafilah* Worships, since the *'ulama'*, learned, have disagreed about the questions, whether (a) *nafilah* Worships may have Substitution performances, and (b) whenever one performs a Worship similar to a *nafilah* that has escaped him, that is a Substitution performance of a Payment. So, when dislike is negated by the weakest of causes, much more is it true that it is negated by entering a mosque, which is a strong cause. For that reason the Worship at funeral is not disliked whenever it comes, and neither is the Worship of the Eclipse and of the Request for Rain, at these times, since they have causes.

The second lesson is the Substitution of the *nafilah* Worship, since the Messenger of Allah performed that. We have, in regard to it, a fine example. 'A'ishah said, "The Messenger of Allah, whenever sleep or illness overcame him, so that he did not rise that night, used to perform a Worship of twelve *rak'ahs* at the first part of the day."

The learned have said, "Whoever is at *nafilah* Worship, and has the response to the *mu'adhdhin* escape him, should perform the Substitute of it, and give the response when he says the Salutation, even though the *mu'adhdhin* has stopped. There is now no meaning to the objection of anyone who says, "That is like the first case, and he does not give a Substitute response;" since, were this objection true, the Messenger of Allah would not have performed them as a Worship in a disliked time. Yes, indeed, whoever has a *wird*, Devotional Recital, to perform and has some excusable thing hinder him from it, should not permit himself to omit it, but should make it up at some other time, so that he may not incline himself to ease and comfort, for some goodwill overtake him in the way of the warfare of the soul and also because Muhammad said, "The deed most liked before Allah is the most constant one, even though it be small." So he should purpose by that method not to be remiss in persevering in his deed.

'A'ishah related from the Prophet that he said, "Allah hates, whoever serves and worships Allah and then abandons his religious service." So then, let him beware of entering under the threat.

The thing confirmed by this tradition is that Allah hated him, and he abandoned it out of weariness, for were it not for the hatred of Allah and his separation (from the mercy of Allah[263]), weariness would not have overcome him.

The fifth is the two *Rak'ahs* after the *wudu*, Ablution. They are liked because the ablution is a means of access, the purpose of which is the Worship, while the defilements are hindrance, for many a time the defilements happens to occur before the Worship, so the state of ablution is broken, and the endeavour is lost. Hastening to the Two *Rak'ahs* is a paying of the purpose of the ablution before it passes away.

That it is liked is known from the tradition of Bilal, since Muhammad said, "I entered the Garden and then saw Bilal in it, so I said to Bilal, 'By what means did you precede me to the Garden?' So Bilal answered, 'I do not know of anything except that I do not perform a new ablution without performing a Worship after it of two *rak'ahs*.'"

The sixth is the Worship of two *rak'ahs* upon Entering the House and upon Leaving it. Abu Salmah[264] related from Abu Hurairah: "He said, 'The Messenger of Allah said, "When you leave your house perform a Worship of two *rak'ahs* which will protect you from the exit of evil, and when you enter the House, perform a Worship of two *rak'ahs* which will protect you from the entrance of evil." ' " This means that every event of importance should begin with it. For this reason, there have come down two *rak'ahs* at the time of the *ihram* (in the Pilgrimage, or minor pilgrimage) and two *rak'ahs* at the beginning of a journey, and two *rak'ahs* upon returning from a journey, in the mosque before entering the house, since all that is handed down as the practice of the Messenger of Allah.

Some of the righteous, whenever they ate anything, used to perform a Worship of two *rak'ahs*, and when they drank anything, to perform a Worship of two *rak'ahs*, and so in everything that happened to them. It is fitting that one should seek the blessing

---

263. This is added by Sayyid Murtada.
264. Abu Salamah b. 'Abd al-Rahman b. 'Awf, *faqih* and imam (d. 94 A.H.).

of Allah at the beginning of things by the mention of Allah. They, the beginnings of things, are of three orders: one of them is repeated frequently, as eating and drinking, so he beings it with "In the name of Allah." Muhammad said, "Every matter of importance that is not begun with 'In the name of Allah the Merciful and Compassionate,' is maimed." The second order is that which is not of frequent occurrence, but which has importance, such as the contracting of marriage, and the beginning of advice and counsel, and then the liked thing in that is that it should be preceded by "The Praise of Allah". Then the one who does the marrying says, "Praise belongs to Allah," and "I invoke a blessing upon the Messenger of Allah. I have married you to my daughter." The one who receives her says, "The praise belongs to Allah," and "I invoke a blessing upon the Messenger of Allah. I have accepted this marriage." It was the custom of the Companions in the beginning of the execution of a message, and the giving of advice and counsel to say the Praise first. The third is that order which does not occur frequently but, when it does occur, has permanence and has importance, such as a journey, and the purchase of a new house, and the act of *ihram*, "separation," and similar things. Then it is liked to do two *rak'ahs* on account of it first. The least important of them is the leaving of the house and entering it, for they are a kind of short journey and return.

The seventh is the Worship for Prospering. Whoever is anxious about a matter, and does not know how it will end, and does not know whether it is better to leave it or to proceed upon it, has been commanded by the Messenger of Allah to perform a Worship of two *rak'ahs* apart from the Prescribed, reciting in the first the Fatihat al-Kitab, and "Say, O ye unbelievers" (cix.), and in the second the Fatihah" and "Say, He is Allah, One" (cxii.), and then, when he finishes, to make his supplication, and say, "O Allah, I ask of Thee prospering by Thy knowledge, and ask Thee to give me power by Thy power, and I ask Thee of Thy great favour, for verily, Thou hast power and I do not have power, and Thou dost know, and I do not know, and Thou art the Knower of the unseen. O Allah, if Thou dost know that this matter is the best for me, in my religion and this life of mine, and the end of this matter of mine, both soon and late, bring it to pass for me, and bless me in it, and then make it easy for me. If Thou dost know that this affair will be bad for me in my religion and this life of mine, and likewise its end, both soon and late, turn me away from it and turn it away from me, and bring to pass for me the best, wherever it may be. Verily Thou art powerful over everything!" Jabir b. 'Abdallah related it. He said, "The Messenger of Allah used to reach us the Worship of Prospering in all affairs, as he used to teach us the *surah.*

Muhammad said, "Whenever any one of you is anxious about an affair, let him perform a Worship of two *rak'ahs,* Then let him mention the affair, and offer a supplication according to what we have mentioned."

The eight is the Worship of Need. Whenever a man's breast oppresses him and necessity in what is beneficial in his religion and this life constrains him to a matter hard for him, let him perform this Worship, for it was related from Wuhaib b. al-Ward[265] that he said, "Among the supplications which are not refused is this, that a creature should perform twelve *rak'ahs,* reciting in each *rak'ah* the Mother of the Book (i.), and the Verse of the Throne (ii. 256), and 'Say, He is Allah, One' (cxii.), and when he finishes, bows down in prostration and then says, "O the Praise of Him Who wears might as a garment," and says in it, "O the Praise of Him Who wraps Himself in glory, and is bountiful in it! O the Praise of Him Who numbers everything by His knowledge! O the Praise of Him to Whom alone Praise belongs! O the Praise of the Possessors of boon and favour! O the Praise of the Possessor of Power! I ask Thee, by the mighty articulations of Thy Throne, and the utmost degree of mercy of Thy Book and by Thy greatest name, and Thy highest greatness, and Thy universal, perfect Words, which no righteous one or sinner passes beyond, to bless Muhammad and the family of Muhammad,' and then asks his need which has no disobedience in it, and he will be answered, if Allah will."

Wuhaib said, "It has reached us that it used to be said, 'Do not teach it to your unintelligent people, for they will assist one another by means of it in disobedience to Allah.' "

One of the wise has said, "Whoever gives four *rak'ahs* is not

---

265. Abu Umayyah Wuhaib b. al-Ward (d. 153 A.H.).

denied four; whoever gives thanks is not denied increase; and whoever gives repentance is not denied acceptance; and whoever gives the Worship of Prospering is not denied good; and whoever gives counsel is not denied correctness."

The ninth is the Worship of the Praise. This Worship is transmitted by Tradition to be done at random, and does not belong to any particular time or any particular occasion. It is liked that the week should not be free from it one time, or the month once, for 'Ikrimah has related from Ibn 'Abbas that Muhamamd said to 'Abbas b. 'Abd al-Muttalib, "Do I not present you, do I not grant you, do I not give you something for which Allah forgives you your sin when you do it, first and last, old and new, mistaken and intentional, secret and open? You perform a Worship of four *rak'ahs,* reciting in every *rak'ah* the Fatihat al-Kitab and another *surah,* and when you finish the Recital in the first *rak'ah* while you are standing, you say, 'O the Praise of Allah!' and 'The Praise belongs to Allah!' and There is no god but Allah!' and 'Allah is greater!' fifteen times. Then you bow and then say them ten times while bowing. Then you raise your head and say them ten times. Then you prostrate and say them ten times. Then you raise your head and say them ten times sitting. Then you prostrate and say them ten times. Then you raise your head and say them ten times, and that makes seventy-five times in every *rak'ah.* You should do that in the four *rak'ahs.* If you are able to perform it every day, do so. But if you do not do it everyday, then on every Friday once. But if you do not do so, then in every year once."

In another tradition it states that one should say in the first *rak'ah* of the Worship, "Thine is the Praise. O Allah!" and "By Thy Praise!" and "Thy name is blessed!" and "Thy greatness is exalted!" "and "Thy names are Hallowed! and "There is no God but Thee!" Then he says the Praise (i.) fifteen times before the Recital and ten times after the Recital, and the rest as has preceded, ten each, and does not say the Praise (i.) after the Prostration while sitting down. This the most beautiful, and it is the choice of Ibn Mubarak.[266] The sum of the two narratives is three hundred

266. Abu 'Abd al-Rahman 'Abdallah b. Mubarak b. Wadih al-Hanzali (cd. 181 A.H) celebrated jurisconsult and ascetic.

Praises. If he performs them in the daytime he does it with one Salutation. If he does it at night, then to do it with two Salutation is better, since it appears that the Worship at night should be by twos. If he adds after the Praise, His saying, "There is no power and no strength but in Allah the High, the Great," that is well, for that has come down in some of the narratives.

Now these are the Worships that have been handed down. None of these *nafilah*, Supererogatory, Worships is liked in the disliked times, except the Worship of the Greeting of the Mosque. As for what we have set forth after the Greeting of the Mosque about the Two *Rak'ahs* of the Ablution, and the Worship of the Journey and the Leaving of the House and the Prospering, they are not allowable, for the prohibition against them is confirmed, and these causes are weak and do not reach the degree of importance of the Eclipse, and the Request for Rain, and the Greeting of the Mosque.

I have seen someone of this Sufis performing the Two *Rak'ahs* of the Ablution in the disliked time, and it is utterly absurd, for the ablution is not the cause for the Worship, but, rather, the Worship is the cause for the ablution. So it is fitting that he should perform the ablution for the Worship, not that he should perform the Worship because he does the ablution, for it would then be the case that everyone who has defiled himself who wishes to perform a Worship in a disliked time, would only have to do the ablution, and perform the Worship, and then there would remain no meaning to dislike.

It is not fitting that he should state the Intention to perform the Two *Rak'ahs* of the Ablution as he states the Intention to perform the Two *Rak'ahs* of the Greeting of the Mosque. Rather when he does the ablution, he performs *tatawwu,'* Voluntary, *rak'ahs* in order that his ablution may not be unemployed, as Bilal used to do, for it is indeed purely voluntary, occurring after the ablution.

The tradition of Bilal does not indicate that the ablution is a cause for the Worship, like the Eclipse and the Greeting of the Mosque, so that he should state the Intention to perform the Two *Rak'ahs* or the Ablution. So it is absurd that he should state the intention to perform the Worship of the Ablution. Rather he states the Intention by the ablution, and what kind of an arrangement is it for him to say in his ablution, "I do the ablution for the sake of my Worship," and then also in his Worship say, "I perform the Worship for the sake of my ablution"? Rather, let him who desires to guard his ablution from becoming unused in a disliked time state the Intention of a Substitution performance, if, by any possibility, there should be incumbent upon him some Worship to which some defect has found its way from some cause or other, for the Substitution performance of the Worship in the disliked times is not disliked.

But as for the stating of the Intention of a *tatawwu'*, Voluntary, Worship: this has no consideration, for in the prohibition against the Worship in the disliked times, there are three important points. One of them is guarding against the resemblance of the worshippers of the sun. The second is guarding against the satan's dispersal, since the Messenger of Allah said, "Verily the sun rises and the horn of Satan is with it, for whenever the sun rises, he is in conjunction with it, and then, when it is high, he leaves it, and then when it is at meridian, he is in conjunction with it, and then, when it passes the meridian, he leaves it, and then when it is near its setting, he is in conjunction with it, and then when it sets, he leaves it." So there is prohibition against the Worship in those times, and attention is drawn by the prohibition to the underlying cause. The third is that those walking the way of the next abode do not cease to continue in the Worship at all times. Continuance in one sort of religious service is what brings on weariness. Whenever one is kept away from it for a time, alacrity increases and incitements spring up, seeing that "man is covetous of what is forbidden."

So in not using these times for the Worship there is increase of incitement and of instigation to await the end of the time. For these times are especially appointed for Praise and Seeking Forgiveness, guarding against weariness that comes through perseverance in one kind of Worship, and seeking relief by changing from one kind of religious service to another, for, in finding a thing to be new and in seeking a new thing there is pleasure and alacrity, while in continuance upon one thing there is heaviness and weariness. For that reason the Worship is not Prostration solely and not Bowing solely, and not Standing solely, but the religious services are organised from a variety of acts and dissimilar forms of Invocations, for the heart secures from each of them a new pleasure upon changing to it. But were it to continue upon one thing, weariness would quickly come upon it. Now if these are matters important in the prohibition against the disliked times, and there are other mysteries, which it is not in the power of man to gaze into, although Allah and His Messenger know better about them, these important things are not to be abandoned except for causes important in the religious law, such as the Substitute performance of the Worship and the Worship of the Request for Rain and of the Eclipse and of the Greeting of the Mosque. As for what is weaker than these, it is not fitting that one should thwart the purpose of the prohibition by them. This is the more regarded opinion, and Allah knows better than anyone else what is correct.

APPENDIX

TABLE OF THE NUMBER OF *RAK'AHS* IN THE DIFFERENT WORSHIPS

I. DAILY:

(a) The *fard* Prescribed Worships and the *ratibah* Fixed Worships connected with them

	rawatib before the Prescribed; *mu'wakkadah*, Confirmed;	*mustahabb*, Liked;	Prescribed;	*rawatib* after the Prescribed; Confirmed;	Liked,
Morning		2 (or after	2		
Noon	2		4	2	
Afternoon	4		4		
Sunset		2 (or after)	2		4
Evening		4			

(b) Other Daily *nafl*, Supererogatory, Worships, all Confirmed:

Witr, Odd	1 to 13
Forenoon	4, 6 or 8
Between the Two Evening Worships	6

II. Weekly:

	Friday	Saturday	Sunday	Monday	Tuesday	Wednesday	Thursday
(a) Daytime	2,4,8 or 12	4	4	2 or 12	10	12	2
(b) Night	12 or 10	12	20	4	2	2,16 or 6	2

III. Yearly:

	Feasts of *al-Fitr*	and *al-Adha*	Ramadan	Rajab	Sha'ban
Confirmed	2	2	20		
Liked				12	100

IV. Occasional:

Eclipse	Request for Rain	Funeral	Greeting of Mosque	Ablution	Entering Mouse, etc.	Prospering	Need	Praise
2	2		2	2	2	2	12	4

Select Bibliography

1. *Encyclopaedias*

Brockelmann, von Karl, *Geschichte der Arabischen Litteratur,* Weimar, 1898, 1902

Encyclopaedia of Islam, Leyden, 1913

Hughes, T.P., *Dictionary of Islam,* London, 1885

Nicholson, R.A., *A Literary History of the Arabs*, London, 1907

2. *Lexicons*

Dozy, R., *Supplement aux Dictionnaires Arabes,* .Leyde, 1881 al-Fairuzabadi, Muhammad b. Ya'qub, *Qamus al-Muhit,* Cairo, 1301

Jayakar, A.S.G., *Ad-Damiri's Hayat al-Hayawan,* London, 1908 Jurjani, *Definitions Viri meritissimi Sejjid Scherif Ali ben Mohammad Dschordschani,* edidit Gustavus Flugel, Lipsiae, 1845.

Lane, E.W., *An Arabic English Lexicon,* 1863

Lisan al'Arab

Murtada, Saiyid Muhammad, *Sharh al-Qamus al-musamma Taj al-'Arus,* Misr, 1306

Smith, R. Payne, *Thesaurus Syriacus*, Oxford, 1901

Sprenger, A., R.W. Nassau Lees, *Dictionary of the Technical Terms,* Calcutta, 1862

al-Zamakhshari, Abu Qasim Mahmud b. 'Umar, *Kitab al-Fa'iq*, Cairo, 1324

3. *Grammars*

De Sacy, M. le Baron Silvestre, *Anthologie Grammmaticale Arabe*, Paris, 1829

Mehren, von A.F., *Die Rhetorik der Araber,* Kopenhagen, 1853

Al-Mufassal, Opus de re Grammatico Arabicum, auctore Abu'l Kasim Mahmud bin 'Omar Zamahsario, edidit J.P. Broch, editio altera, Christianiae, 1940

Rechendrof, von H, *Arabische Syntax*, Heidelberg, 1921

4. *Theology*

Commentary of Ibrahim al-Bajuri, on the Text of Abu Shuja', Cairo, 1303

Macdonald D.B., *Development of Muslim Theology, Jurisprudence and Constitutional Theroy*, New York, 1903

Macdonald, D.B., *The Religious Attitude and Life in Islam*, Chicago, 1909

Sell, E., *The Faith of Islam*, London, 1896

5. *Commentaries on Qur'an and Traditions*

'Abduh, Muhammad, *Tafsir al-Fatihah*, Cairo, 1330

Abu Sa'id Abdallah b. 'Umar al-Baidawi, *Anwar al-Tanzil wa Asrar al-Ta'wil*, edidit H.O. Fleischer, 2 vols., Lipsiae, 1846-48

Chrestomathia Baidawiana, the commentary of El-Baidawi on Sura III, by D.S. Margoliouth, London 1894

al-Khatib al-Tabrizi, Muhammad b.. 'Abdallah, *Mishkat al-Masabih*, Cairo, 1309

Kitab al-Misbah al-Munir fi Gharib al-Sharh al-Kabir, iii-Rafi'i, ta'lif Ahmad b. Muhammad al-Faiumi, 2 vols., 1315, 1316

al-Qastallani, Ahmad b Muhammad, *Irshad al-Sari ila Sharh Sahih al-Bukhari*, Cairo, 1304-1305

6. *History*

Annales Quos Scripsit Abu Djafar Mohammad Ibn Djarir at-Tabari, cum aliis edidit K.J. De Goeje, Ludg., Bat., 1879-1901

Muir, Sir William, *The Caliphate, Its Rise, Decline and Fall*, rev. edn. by T.H. Weir, Edinburgh, 1915

Noldeke, Theodor, *Sketches from Eastern History*. Trans. J.S. Black, London 1892

7. *Biographies*

Abu al-Hasan Ali b. al-Athir, *Tajrid Asma' al-Sahabah*, Hyderabad Deccan, 1315

De Slane, Bn Mac Guckin, *Ibn Khallikan's Biographical Dictionary*, 4 vols., Paris, 1842, 1871

Ibn Hajar, *A Biographical Dictionary of Persons who knew Mohammad,* Calcutta, 1856, 4 vols.

Ibn Nadim, *Kitab al-Fihrist,* herausgegeben von Gustav Flugel, Leipzig, 1871-72

al-Jabarti, 'Abd al-Rahman b. al-Shaikh Hasan, *'Aja'ib al-Athar fi'l-Taradjim wa'l-Akhbar*, Bulaq, 1297, 4 vols.

Margoliouth, D.S., Ed., *Irshad al-Arib ila Ma'rifat al-Adib* (or *Dictionary of Learned Men of Yaqut*), Leyden, 1907-13

Sprenger, A., and Mawlawi 'Abd al-Haqq, *Tusy's Index (Fihris Tusi) of Shi'ah Books*, Calcutta, 1853

8. *General*

Burton, Sir R.H., *Personal Narrative of a Pilgrimage to al Madinah and Mecca,* London, 1893

Lane, E.W., *The Manners and Customs of the modern Egyptians,* London

9. *Al-Ghazzali*

Gardner, W.R.W., *Al-Ghazali,* Madras, 1919

Gautier, L, *Ad-Do'ufra al-Fakhira la Perle Precieuse de Ghazzali,* Geneve, 1878

Macdonald, D.B., "The Life of Ghazzali," *Journal of the American Oriental Society*, Vol. XX, 1899

Zwemer, Samuel M., *A Moslem Seeker after God,* New York, 1920

